Searching Through the Teachings of Jesus - - -

So as to Implant Them into Your Heart

Compiled and Presented By:
Fr. Stephen Valenta, OFM Conv.

IMPRIMI POTEST:
>Fr. Canice Connors, OFM Conv.
>Minister Provincial

NIHIL OBSTAT:
>Francis J. McAree, S.T.D.
>Censor Librorum

IMPRIMATUR:
>+The Most Reverend Robert A. Brucato, D.D.
>Vicar General, Archdiocese of New York
>October 11, 2000

The Nihil Obstat and Imprimatur are official declarations that a book or pamphlet is free of doctrinal or moral error. No implication in contained that those who have granted the Nihil Obstat and Imprimatur agree with the contents, opinions or statements expressed.

Library of Congress Control No.:   00-140039
ISBN: 0-9705979-0-8

Printed in the USA

In Appreciation

In my dreams it seemed that it would be a simple task. In reality, it was not. I wish to express a depth of gratitude to Eileen Gallo, Sister Louis Marie, and to William and Kathleen Roesch. This book would not have been compiled and written were it not for their dedicated assistance. May the Lord reward them with an abundance of graces.

Table of Contents

Foreword

Leave it to Father Stephen Valenta to surface a spiritually enriching concept that has long been seeking expression.

This latest effort of a devoted Conventual Franciscan friar shouldn't come as a surprise to those who know him. His zeal to pass on Christ's teaching, together with a deeper understanding of it, has been this friar's trademark for some few decades. As a friend once remarked, "Father Stephen isn't satisfied with that which is simply satisfactory; his aim is to elevate the understanding of Christ's teaching to a level that will dispose readers to exclaim, "Now the Scriptures are coming alive".

Indeed, "Searching Through the Teachings of Jesus" achieves exactly that. To be sure, any serious-minded person who is seeking spiritual enrichment can only profit greatly from Father Stephen's comprehensive effort. It is alive! It reflects Christ's deepest teachings in a manner that not only elevate the reader's *understanding* of Our Master's thoughts and words but, as well, it takes dead aim at the heart.

How many a religious-minded person said, "I love my Bible and I try to integrate it into my life. But, to tell the truth, I'm not sure I'm my best guide". Well, here's the answer. The tome in question makes not only for enlightened reading but, as well, it is such that it touches the heart. And wasn't that Christ's very aim in extending His Word to us?

Dear reader, enjoy! You have a treat awaiting you within the pages that follow. Our Lord said, "Come to Me, you who labor and are burdened and I will refresh you". Well, here's your opportunity. And it won't stop there. No, not at all! You will now be better equipped to bring Christ and His teachings and lessons of love into the lives of others. What a blessing! What an opportunity! As the younger element of our society might say, "GO FOR IT"!

Father Edgar Holden, OFM Conv.
St. Francis Friary
Staten Island, NY

Preface

For many years, as a Franciscan priest, I have taught the faithful whether as individuals, within the framework of days of recollection, parish missions, and workshops on prayer. One of the recommendations I have always made that would increase the fruits of my teaching, was that they take the Gospel of St. Matthew and just highlight the teachings of Jesus. Once they had done this, then they were to go to the Gospel of St. John and do the same. Within the contents of these two Gospels they would come up with the bulk of what Jesus taught. In following through on this recommendation, they would have at their fingertips what they had to do to become true followers of Jesus, that is, to become thoroughly Christian.

After presenting this suggestion to thousands of the faithful, and taking a sample of fifty or so, I found out that it was too difficult for one reason or another for them to bind themselves to the above recommendation. What to do, to make it more possible for more of the faithful, to avail themselves of the full body of Jesus' teaching? The answer came in prayer: pull out the teachings of Jesus yourself, and then in crystal form make them available to them in book form with an additional simplification now and then. Doing it this way made it possible for me to pull the teachings of Jesus out from the complete four Gospels.

The hardship of doing this is now evident to me. The chapters are many, the time is pressing to fulfill many other responsibilities not found within the "free to do or not" department. People at large know the things that Jesus DID and remember them well. The things that Jesus did are more plentiful that the things which He SAID. The things which He said are much more difficult to remember. This goes without saying.

It is my opinion presenting this volume of the teachings of Jesus will be most helpful. Having the teachings in their original, and having them directly from Jesus Himself, will make it that much easier to take them bit by bit, thought by thought, subject by subject, and put them into practice. Those particular instructions that I felt were given to the Apostles themselves for logistical purposes, are not included.

To know the teachings of Jesus is one thing; to put them into practice is another. To make these teachings more easily available, with grace, they can be blended into one's daily life with greater ease and with lasting fruits.

As in the days when Jesus walked in the midst of the people, He was under the loving care of the Holy Spirit, it is recommended to the reader first to pray to the Holy Spirit for guidance and then, and only then, to pursue in thought and heart, first to get to know the teachings and ultimately to place them within the caresses of one's heart for safe keeping and implementing.

All Scriptural quotes have been taken from "The New American Bible" (Revised Edition).

Searching Through the Teachings of Jesus - ~ ~

As Found in the Gospel of St. Matthew

So as to Implant Them into Your Heart

Chapter 4:

One does not live by bread alone, / but by every word that comes forth from the mouth of God. (4)

In addition to food for the body, one needs food for the soul.

Repent, for the kingdom of heaven is at hand. (17)

Turn back to God to be able to enter into His Kingdom.

Chapter 5:

Blessed are the poor in spirit, / for theirs is the kingdom of heaven.

Be detached from your own thoughts, your own wishes, yourself.

Blessed are they who mourn, / for they will be comforted.

In your sorrow, you will be comforted.

Blessed are the meek, / for they will inherit the land.

Be meek.

Blessed are they who hunger and thirst for righteousness, / for they will be satisfied.

Hunger and thirst for that which is right.

Blessed are the merciful,/for they will be shown mercy.

Show mercy to others.

Blessed are the clean of heart, /for they will see God.

You are to have a clean heart.

Blessed are the peacemakers, / for they will be called children of God.

Be a peacemaker.

Blessed are they who are persecuted for the sake of righteousness, / for theirs is the kingdom of heaven.

Allow yourself to be persecuted for that which is right.

Blessed are you when they insult you and persecute you and

Allow yourself to be persecuted and maligned because you are a

utter every kind of evil against you [falsely] because of me. Rejoice and be glad, for your reward will be great in heaven. ₅ Thus they persecuted the prophets who were before you. (3 – 12)

follower of Jesus.

You are the salt of the earth. ₁₀ But if salt loses its taste, with what can it be seasoned? It is no longer good for anything but to be thrown out and trampled underfoot. (13)

You are they who are to preserve goodness on the earth.

₁₅

You are the light of the world. A city set on a mountain cannot be hidden. Nor do they light a lamp and then put it ₂₀ under a bushel basket; it is set on a lamp stand, where it gives light to all in the house. Just so, your light must shine before others, that they may see your ₂₅ good deeds and glorify your heavenly Father. (14 – 16)

You are to manifest truth to the world and give good example.

Do not think that I have come to abolish the law or the proph-₃₀ ets. I have come not to abolish but to fulfill. Amen, I say to you, until heaven and earth pass away, not the smallest letter or the smallest part of a letter will ₃₅ pass from the law, until all things have taken place. (17– 18)

Do not think that I have come to rid the world of the laws of the Old Testament or cancel out the words of the prophets. These still hold and will hold till what is in the law or what the prophets spoke will have taken place.

Therefore, whoever breaks one of the least of these com-₄₀ mandments and teaches others to do so will be called least in the kingdom of heaven. But

Whoever breaks the least of these commandments and teaches others to do the same, will be called least in the kingdom of heaven. On the other whoever obeys and teaches these commandments will be called greatest in the kingdom of heaven. I tell you, unless your righteousness surpasses that of the scribes and Pharisees, you will not enter into the kingdom of heaven. (19 - 20)

You have heard that it was said to your ancestors, 'You shall not kill; and whoever kills will be liable to judgment.' But I say to you, whoever is angry with his brother will be liable to judgment, and whoever says to his brother, 'Raqa,' will be answerable to the Sanhedrin, and whoever says, 'You fool,' will be liable to fiery Gehenna. Therefore, if you bring your gift to the altar, and there recall that your brother has anything against you, leave your gift there at the altar, go first and be reconciled with your brother, and then come and offer your gift.
(21 – 24)

Settle with your opponent quickly while on the way to court with him. Otherwise your opponent will hand you over to the judge, and the judge will hand you over to the guard, and you will be thrown into prison. Amen, I say to you, you will not be released until you have paid the last penny. (25 – 26)

You have heard that it was said, 'You shall not commit

hand, whoever obeys them and teaches others to do the same will be called greatest in the kingdom of heaven. I tell you, unless your goodness goes beyond that of the Pharisees, you will not enter heaven. 5

There will be a serious punishment for one who is angry with, or ridicules or demeans another. 10

15

20

If you attempt to give due service to God and recall that someone has something against you, you must first reconcile with that person and only after 25 that continue to give your due service to God.

Settle with your opponent before he begins to take serious 30 action against you. If you do not, you can expect even more serious consequences.

35

40

Anyone who lusts after another is already guilty of an adulterous

adultery.' But I say to you, everyone who looks at a woman with lust has already committed adultery with her in his heart.
(27 – 28)

act within one's heart even if there was no physical expression of the lust.

If your right eye causes you to sin, tear it out and throw it away. It is better for you to lose one of your members than to have your whole body thrown into Gehenna. And if your right hand causes you to sin, cut it off and throw it away. It is better for you to lose one of your members than to have your whole body go into Gehenna.
(29 – 30)

One must ruthlessly root out every occasion of sin otherwise he/she is placed into a serious condition of losing his/her soul.

It was also said, 'Whoever divorces his wife must give her a bill of divorce.' But I say to you, whoever divorces his wife (unless the marriage is unlawful) causes her to commit adultery, and whoever marries a divorced woman commits adultery.
(31 – 32)

Whoever divorces one's spouse, (except in the case when a marriage is unlawful) causes the other to commit adultery as also the one who marries the divorced spouse.

Again you have heard that it was said to your ancestors, 'Do not take a false oath, but make good to the Lord all that you vow.' But I say to you, do not swear at all; not by heaven, for it is God's throne; nor by the earth, for it is his footstool; nor by Jerusalem, for it is the city of the great King. Do not swear by your head, for you cannot make a single hair white or black. Let your 'Yes' mean 'Yes,' and your

Do not lie in taking an oath. If you take an oath be sure that you are telling the truth.

Say 'Yes' when you mean 'Yes,'

No' mean 'No.' Anything more is from the evil one. (33 – 37)

You have heard that it was said, 'An eye for an eye and a tooth for a tooth.' But I say to you, offer no resistance to one who is evil. When someone strikes you on [your] right cheek, turn the other one to him as well. If anyone wants to go to law with you over your tunic, hand him your cloak as well. Should anyone press you into service for one mile, go with him for two miles. Give to the one who asks of you, and do not turn your back on one who wants to borrow. (38 – 42)

You have heard that it was said, 'You shall love your neighbor and hate your enemy.' But I say to you, love your enemies, and pray for those who persecute you, that you may be children of your heavenly Father, for he makes his sun rise on the bad and the good, and causes rain to fall on the just and the unjust. For if you love those who love you, what recompense will you have? Do not the tax collectors do the same? And if you greet your brothers only, what is unusual about that? Do not the pagans do the same? So be perfect, just as your heavenly Father is perfect. (43 – 48)

Chapter 6

and 'No' when you mean 'No.' Anything more is from the evil one.

5

Offer no resistance to one who is evil. In fact, give of yourself even more than that which is 10 demanded of you.

15

Give to those who ask you for help in their need and do not hesitate in loaning to those who ask to borrow from you.

20

You are to love your enemy and pray for those who persecute you. You are to love him for WHO he is, a PERSON created to the image and likeness of 25 God. His hate, meanness, even if he chooses to put you to death, all fall into the category of WHATS. You have the example of the heavenly Father 30 Who loves even those who do not love Him.

35

You are to be perfect as your heavenly Father is perfect.

40

[But] take care not to perform righteous deeds in order that people may see them; otherwise, you will have no recompense from your heavenly Father. When you give alms, do not blow a trumpet before you, as the hypocrites do in the synagogues and in the streets to win the praise of others. Amen, I say to you, they have received their reward. But when you give alms, do not let your left hand know what your right is doing, so that your almsgiving may be secret. And your Father who sees in secret will repay you.

When you pray, do not be like the hypocrites, who love to stand and pray in the synagogues and on street corners so that others may see them. Amen, I say to you, they have received their reward. But when you pray, go to your inner room, close the door, and pray to your Father in secret. And your Father who sees in secret will repay you. (1 – 6)

When you do what is good, such as give alms or pray to the Father, be careful not to allow yourselves to do these so that people would see and give you praise. Whatever you do, do it in secret, privately, so that the Father, Who sees what you do, would be the one Who would reward you.

In praying, do not babble like the pagans, who think that they will be heard because of their many words. Do not be like them. Your Father knows what you need before you ask him. This is how you are to pray: / Our Father in heaven, / hallowed be your name / your kingdom come, / your will be done, / on earth as in heaven. / Give us today our daily bread;

When you pray do not think that the use of many words will win a hearing. Your Father knows what you need before you ask Him.

This is how you are to pray: Our Father in heaven, hallowed be your name, your kingdom come, your will be done, on earth as in heaven. Give us today our daily bread; and forgive

/ and forgive us our debts, / as we forgive our debtors; / and do not subject us to the final test, / but deliver us from the evil one. (7 – 13)

If you forgive others their transgressions, your heavenly Father will forgive you. But if you do not forgive others, neither will your Father forgive your transgressions.

When you fast, do not look gloomy like the hypocrites. They neglect their appearance, so that they may appear to others to be fasting. Amen, I say to you, they have received their reward. But when you fast, anoint your head and wash your face, so that you may not appear to be fasting, except to your Father who is hidden. And your Father who sees what is hidden will repay you.

Do not store up for yourselves treasures on earth, where moth and decay destroys, and thieves break in and steal. But store up treasures in heaven, where neither moth nor decay destroy, nor thieves break in and steal. For where your treasure is, there also will your heart be. (14 – 21)

The lamp of the body is the eye. If your eye is sound, your whole body will be filled with light; but if your eye is bad, your whole body will be in darkness. And if the light in you is darkness, how great will the darkness be. (22 – 23)

our debts, as we forgive our debtors; and do not subject us to the final test, but deliver us from the evil one.

5

If you forgive others their transgressions, your heavenly Father will forgive you. But if you do not forgive others, neither will your Father forgive your transgressions.

10

When you fast let it not be for praise. Let it be done secretly so that you would receive your reward from the Father who sees what is hidden.

15

20

Do not store up your treasures on earth. They can be destroyed or stolen. Instead store up your treasures in heaven where they cannot be destroyed or stolen. This way, your heart will be on the things of heaven instead on the things of earth.

25

30

If the truth is in you, you will enlighten others. If you do not have the truth and you think that your lack of truth is the truth, how great will the lack of truth be.

35

40

No one can serve two masters. He will either hate one and love the other, or be devoted to one and despise the other. You can-
5 not serve God and mammon.

(24)

No one can worship God and money at the same time. It is either one or the other. There is no in between.

Therefore I tell you, do not worry about your life, what you
10 will eat [or drink], or about your body, what you will wear. Is not life more than food and the body more than clothing? Look at the birds in the sky; they do
15 not sow or reap, they gather nothing into barns, yet your heavenly Father feeds them. Are not you more important than they? Can any of you by worry-
20 ing add a single moment to your life-span? Why are you anxious about clothes? Learn from the way the wild flowers grow. They do not work or spin. But I tell
25 you that not even Solomon in all his splendor was clothed like one of them. If God so clothes the grass of the field, which grows today and is thrown into
30 the oven tomorrow, will he not much more provide for you, O you of little faith? So do not worry and say, 'What are we to eat?' or 'What are we to drink?'
35 or 'What are we to wear?' All these things the pagans seek. Your heavenly Father knows that you need them all. But seek first the kingdom [of God] and his
40 righteousness, and all these things will be given you besides. Do not worry about tomorrow;

Do not worry about your life, what you are to eat or wear. Life is worth much more that either of these. The birds and the flowers are taken care of by the Father. You are worth more than these. Trust Him in these matters.

The worldly will worry about worldly things. Your heavenly Father knows that you need the essentials of life. Seek to put Him first in your life, aspire after goodness and all of these will be given to you.

Do not worry about tomorrow;

tomorrow will take care of itself. Sufficient for a day is its own evil. (25 – 34)

Chapter 7

Stop judging, that you may not be judged. For as you judge, so will you be judged, and the measure with which you measure will be measured out to you. (1– 2)

Why do you notice the splinter in your brother's eye, but do not perceive the wooden beam in your own eye? How can you say to your brother, 'Let me remove that splinter from your eye,' while the wooden beam is in your eye? You hypocrite, remove the wooden beam from your eye first; then you will see clearly to remove the splinter from your brother's eye. (3 – 5)

Do not give what is holy to dogs, or throw your pearls before swine, lest they trample them underfoot, and turn and tear you to pieces. (6)

Ask and it will be given to you; seek and you will find; knock and the door will be opened to you. For everyone who asks, receives; and the one who seeks, finds; and to the one who knocks, the door will be opened. Which one of you would hand his son a stone when he asks for a loaf of bread, or a snake when

tomorrow will take care of itself.

Stop judging, that you may not be judged. For as you judge, so will you be judged, and the measure with which you measure will be measured out to you.

Why do you concern yourself with the minor faults of others when you yourself have greater faults. Clean up your act and then you will be of assistance to others to do the same.

Do not share your Faith with those unable to give it the respect that it deserves. In anger they may turn on you and do you harm.

Ask and it will be given to you; seek and you will find; knock and the door will be opened to you. For everyone who asks, receives; and the one who seeks, finds; and to the one who knocks, the door will be opened.

he asks for a fish? If you then, who are wicked, know how to give good gifts to your children, how much more will your heav-
5 enly Father give good things to those who ask him. (7 – 11)

Do to others whatever you would have them do to you.
10 This is the law and the prophets. (12)

Enter through the narrow gate; for the gate is wide and the
15 road broad that leads to destruction, and those who enter through it are many. How narrow the gate and constricted the road that leads to life. And those
20 who find it are few. (13 – 14)

Beware of false prophets, who come to you in sheep's clothing, but underneath are ravenous
25 wolves. By their fruits you will know them. Do people pick grapes from thorn bushes, or figs from thistles? Just so, every good tree bears good fruit, and a rot-
30 ten tree bears bad fruit. A good tree cannot bear bad fruit, nor can a rotten tree bear good fruit. Every tree that does not bear good fruit will be cut down and
35 thrown into the fire. So by their fruits you will know them.
(15 – 20)

Not everyone who says to me,
40 'Lord, Lord,' will enter the kingdom of heaven, but only the one who does the will of my

If those who are wicked know how to give good things to others, how much more will the heavenly Father Who is goodness personified give to you when you ask.

Do to others whatever you would have them do to you.

You are not to take the easy way in life. This leads to destruction. Put forth exertion into your spiritual journey. It is true: Many are they who take the easy way, few who take the path that leads to Heaven.

Beware of those who on the outside seem to be very genial, but on the inside are evil. The way to tell the good from the evil, check on their actions. By their fruits you will know them, the one from the other.

In the same vein those who seem on the outside to be close to the Lord, are not at times truly so. Even though they seem to do

Father in heaven. Many will say to me on that day, 'Lord, Lord, did we not prophesy in your name? Did we not drive out demons in your name? Did we not do mighty deeds in your name?' Then I will declare to them solemnly, 'I never knew you. Depart from me, you evil-doers.' (21 – 23)

Everyone who listens to these words of mine and acts on them will be like a wise man who built his house on rock. The rain fell, the floods came, and the winds blew and buffeted the house. But it did not collapse; it had been set solidly on rock. And everyone who listens to these words of mine but does not act on them will be like a fool who built his house on sand. The rain fell, the floods came, and winds blew and buffeted the house. And it collapsed and was completely ruined. (24 – 27)

Chapter 8

Amen, I say to you, in no one in Israel have I found such faith. I say to you, many will come from the east and the west, and will recine with Abraham, Isaac, and Jacob at the banquet in the kingdom of heaven, but the children of the kingdom will be driven out into the outer darkness, where there will be wailing and grinding of teeth....You may go; as you have believed, let

good things, they do them for their own benefit. Neither they, nor their deeds are pleasing to Him. He will be really stern with them.   5

Everyone who listens to these words and puts them into practice is considered to be a person of wisdom. If he hears them and   15 does not put them into practice. He is indeed a fool.

20

25

30

35

40

it be done for you. (10 – 13)

Foxes have dens and birds of
the sky have nests, but the Son
5 of Man has nowhere to rest his
head. (20)

Follow me, and let the dead
bury their dead. (22)

Make Jesus more important to your
life than anything or anyone else.

10

Chapter 9

Courage, child, your sins are
forgiven.…Why do you harbor
15 evil thoughts? Which is easier,
to say, 'Your sins are forgiven,'
or to say, 'Rise and walk '? But
that you may know that the Son
of Man has authority on earth
20 to forgive sins -- Rise, pick up
your stretcher, and go home.…
                            (2 – 6)

Those who are well do not
25 need a physician, but the sick
do. Go and learn the meaning
of the words, 'I desire mercy, not
sacrifice.' I did not come to call
the righteous but sinners.
30   (12 – 13)

Make mercy in your life more
important than sacrifice.

Can the wedding guests
mourn as long as the bridegroom is with them? The days
35 will come when the bridegroom
is taken away from them, and
then they will fast. No one
patches an old cloak with a piece
of unshrunken cloth, for its full-
40 ness pulls away from the cloak and
the tear gets worse. People do not
put new wine into old wineskins.

Otherwise the skins burst, the wine spills out, and the skins are ruined. Rather, they pour new wine into fresh wineskins, and both are pre served. (15 – 17)

The harvest is abundant but the laborers are few; so ask the master of the harvest to send out laborers for his harvest. (37 – 38)

Pray to the Father and He will send you vocations to be of help to the needy.

Chapter 10

As you go, make this proclamation: 'The kingdom of heaven is at hand.' Cure the sick, raise the dead, cleanse lepers, drive out demons. Without cost you have received; without cost you are to give. Do not take gold or silver or copper for your belts; no sack for the journey, or a second tunic, or sandals, or walking stick. The laborer deserves his keep. Whatever town or village you enter, look for a worthy person in it, and stay there until you leave. As you enter a house, wish it peace. If the house is worthy, let your peace come upon it; if not, let your peace return to you. Whoever will not receive you or listen to your words -- go outside that house or town and shake the dust from your feet. Amen, I say to you, it will be more tolerable for the land of Sodom and Gomorrah on the day of judgment than for that town.

Behold, I am sending you like sheep in the midst of wolves; so be shrewd as serpents and simple

Make use of the power that comes from heaven to provide the needy with physical and spiritual help.

Go out doing good, be simple, but make use of wisdom and prudence.

as doves. But beware of people, for they will hand you over to courts and scourge you in their synagogues, and you will be led
5 before governors and kings for my sake as a witness before them and the pagans. When they hand you over, do not worry about how you are to speak or
10 what you are to say. You will be given at that moment what you are to say. For it will not be you who speak but the Spirit of your Father speaking through you.
15 Brother will hand over brother to death, and the father his child; children will rise up against parents and have them put to death. You will be hated
20 by all because of my name, but whoever endures to the end will be saved. When they persecute you in one town, flee to another. Amen, I say to you, you will not
25 finish the towns of Israel before the Son of Man comes. (7 – 23)

When those who are evil wish not to follow your encouragements to live a life according to the teachings of Jesus, and so begin to manhandle you and cause you harm, rely on the Holy Spirit to speak through you.

If you are persecuted in one town, flee to another.

(Notice the prophesy given here!)

No disciple is above his teacher, no slave above his mas-
30 ter. It is enough for the disciple that he become like his teacher, for the slave that he become like his master. If they have called the master of the house
35 Beelzebub, how much more those of his household!
    Therefore do not be afraid of them. Nothing is concealed that will not be revealed, nor secret
40 that will not be known. What I say to you in the darkness, speak in the light; what you hear whis-

Do not fear those who choose to do you harm. As followers of Jesus expect it.

Do not be afraid of what evil people can do to you. You have great worth with the Father.

Whatever I give to you in knowledge speak of it in the

pered, proclaim on the house-tops. And do not be afraid of those who kill the body but cannot kill the soul; rather, be afraid of the one who can destroy both soul and body in Gehenna. Are not two sparrows sold for a small coin? Yet not one of them falls to the ground without your Father's knowledge. Even all the hairs of your head are counted. So do not be afraid; you are worth more than many sparrows. (24 – 31)

Everyone who acknowledges me before others I will acknowledge before my heavenly Father. But whoever denies me before others, I will deny before my heavenly Father.

Do not think that I have come to bring peace upon the earth. I have come to bring not peace but the sword. For I have come to set / a man 'against his father, / a daughter against her mother, and a daughter-in-law against her mother-in-law; / and one's enemies will be those of his household.' / Whoever loves father or mother more than me is not worthy of me, and whoever loves son or daughter more than me is not worthy of me; and whoever does not take up his cross and follow after me is not worthy of me. Whoever finds his life will lose it, and whoever loses his life for my sake will find it. Whoever receives you receives me, and whoever receives me

open that others might benefit.

Do not fear martyrdom. Fear rather the possibility of losing your soul. [5]

Do not fear what evil can befall you. You have great worth before the Father. [10]

[15]

You are to acknowledge me before others if you wish to be acknowledged by Jesus before His Father.

[20]

Do not put anyone before Jesus. [25]

[30]

To be worthy of Jesus one must take up the hardships of life and be a true disciple.

[35]

Do not put yourself first in life. Instead, give your life over to Jesus and thus you will enjoy its fullness. [40]

receives the one who sent me. Whoever receives a prophet because he is a prophet will receive a prophet's reward, and whoever
5 receives a righteous man because he is righteous will receive a righteous man's reward. And whoever gives only a cup of cold water to one of these little ones to
10 drink because he is a disciple -- amen, I say to you, he will surely not lose his reward. (32 – 42)

Chapter 11

15

Go and tell John what you hear and see: the blind regain their sight, the lame walk, lepers are cleansed, the deaf hear,
20 the dead are raised, and the poor have the good news proclaimed to them. And blessed is the one who takes no offense at me.
                              (4 – 6)
25

What did you go out to the desert to see? A reed swayed by the wind? Then what did you go out to see? Someone dressed
30 in fine clothing? Those who wear fine clothing are in royal palaces. Then why did you go out? To see a prophet? Yes, I tell you, and more than a prophet.
35 This is the one about whom it is written: / 'Behold, I am sending my messenger ahead of you; / he will prepare your way before you.' / Amen, I say to you,
40 among those born of women there has been none greater than John the Baptist; yet the least in

Give due consideration to those who are faithful to Jesus. Doing so, you will not be without a reward.

the kingdom of heaven is greater than he. From the days of John the Baptist until now, the kingdom of heaven suffers violence, and the violent are taking it by force. All the prophets and the law prophesied up to the time of John. And if you are willing to accept it, he is Elijah, the one who is to come. Whoever has ears ought to hear. (7 – 15)

To what shall I compare this generation? It is like children who sit in marketplaces and call to one another, 'We played the flute for you, but you did not dance, we sang a dirge but you did not mourn.' For John came neither eating nor drinking, and they said, 'He is possessed by a demon.' The Son of Man came eating and drinking and they said, 'Look, he is a glutton and a drunkard, a friend of tax collectors and sinners.' But wisdom is vindicated by her works.
                    (16 – 19)

Woe to you, Chorazin! Woe to you, Bethsaida! For if the mighty deeds done in your midst had been done in Tyre and Sidon, they would long ago have repented in sackcloth and ashes. But I tell you, it will be more tolerable for Tyre and Sidon on the Day of Judgment than for you. And as for you, Capernaum: / 'Will you be exalted to heaven? / You will go down to the netherworld.' / For

To be a part in the kingdom of heaven requires an aggressive stance, an aggressive stand.

5

10

15

20

25

30

35

40

if the mighty deeds done in your midst had been done in Sodom, it would have remained until this day. But I tell you, it will be
5 more tolerable for the land of Sodom on the day of judgment than for you. (21 – 24)

I give praise to you, Father,
10 Lord of heaven and earth, for although you have hidden these things from the wise and the learned you have revealed them to the childlike. Yes, Father, such
15 has been your gracious will. All things have been handed over to me by my Father. No one knows the Son except the Father, and no one knows the Father except
20 the Son and anyone to whom the Son wishes to reveal him.

Come to me, all you who labor and are burdened, and I will give you rest. Take my yoke
25 upon you and learn from me, for I am meek and humble of heart; and you will find rest for yourselves. For my yoke is easy, and my burden light. (25 – 30)

30

Chapter 12

Have you not read what David did when he and his com-
35 panions were hungry, how he went into the house of God and ate the bread of offering, which neither he nor his companions but only the priests could law-
40 fully eat? Or have you not read in the law that on the sabbath the priests serving in the temple

Become childlike to be able to receive an understanding of things which are hidden to the wise.

"Come to me all you who labor and are burdened and I will give you rest."

"Learn from me, for I am meek and humble of heart."

violate the sabbath and are innocent? I say to you, something greater than the temple is here. If you knew what this meant, 'I desire mercy, not sacrifice,' you would not have condemned these innocent men. For the Son of Man is Lord of the sabbath. (3 – 8)

"I desire mercy, not sacrifice." 5

Is it lawful to cure on the sabbath?…Which one of you who has a sheep that falls into a pit on the sabbath will not take hold of it and lift it out? How much more valuable a person is than a sheep. So it is lawful to do good on the sabbath.…Stretch out your hand. (11 - 12)

It is lawful to do good on the 10 Lord's Day.

When there is a real need of assisting someone on the Day of the Lord, such an action is ac- 15 ceptable.

Every kingdom divided against itself will be laid waste, and no town or house divided against itself will stand. And if Satan drives out Satan, he is divided against himself; how, then, will his kingdom stand? And if I drive out demons by Beelzebub, by whom do your own people drive them out? Therefore they will be your judges. But if it is by the Spirit of God that I drive out demons, then the kingdom of God has come upon you. How can anyone enter a strong man's house and steal his property, unless he first ties up the strong man? Then he can plunder his house. Whoever is not with me is against me, and whoever does not gather with me scatters. Therefore, I say to you, every sin

Whoever is not with me is 20 against me and whoever does not gather with me scatters.

25

30

35

40

and blasphemy will be forgiven people, but blasphemy against the Spirit will not be forgiven. And whoever speaks a word
5 against the Son of Man will be forgiven; but whoever speaks against the Holy Spirit will not be forgiven, either in this age or in the age to come.

blaspheme the Holy Spirit. This sort of sin will not be forgiven.

10 Either declare the tree good and its fruit is good, or declare the tree rotten and its fruit is rotten, for a tree is known by its fruit. You brood of vipers, how
15 can you say good things when you are evil? For from the fullness of the heart the mouth speaks. A good person brings forth good out of a store of
20 goodness, but an evil person brings forth evil out of a store of evil. I tell you, on the day of judgment people will render an account for every careless word
25 they speak. By your words you will be acquitted, and by your words you will be condemned.
(25 – 37)

(Notice here that Jesus speaks of the age to come.)

From the fullness of the heart the mouth speaks.

On the day of judgment all will have to render an account for every careless words they speak. By way of one's words, one will be either acquitted or condemned.

30 An evil and unfaithful generation seeks a sign, but no sign will be given it except the sign of Jonah the prophet. Just as Jonah was in the belly of the whale
35 three days and three nights, so will the Son of Man be in the heart of the earth three days and three nights. At the judgment, the men of Nineveh will arise
40 with this generation and condemn it, because they repented at the preaching of Jonah; and

there is something greater than Jonah here. At the judgment the queen of the south will arise with this generation and condemn it, because she came from the ends of the earth to hear the wisdom of Solomon; and there is something greater than Solomon here.

When an unclean spirit goes out of a person it roams through arid regions searching for rest but finds none. Then it says, 'I will return to my home from which I came.' But upon returning, it finds it empty, swept clean, and put in order. Then it goes and brings back with itself seven other spirits more evil than itself, and they move in and dwell there; and the last condition of that person is worse than the first. Thus it will be with this evil generation. (39 – 45)

Who is my mother? Who are my brothers?…Here are my mother and my brothers. For whoever does the will of my heavenly Father is my brother, and sister, and mother. (48 – 50)

Chapter 13

A sower went out to sow. And as he sowed, some seed fell on the path, and birds came and ate it up. Some fell on rocky ground, where it had little soil. It sprang up at once because the soil was not deep, and when the sun rose it was scorched, and it

Caution must be exercised after one's conversion that one does not fall into a deeper state of sin than one was in before one's conversion.

withered for lack of roots. Some seed fell among thorns, and the thorns grew up and choked it. But some seed fell on rich soil,
5 and produced fruit, a hundred or sixty or thirtyfold. Whoever has ears ought to hear.... To anyone who has, more will be given and he will grow rich; from any-
10 one who has not, even what he has will be taken away. This is why I speak to them in parables, because 'they look but do not see and hear but do not listen
15 or understand.' Isaiah's prophecy is fulfilled in them, which says: / 'You shall indeed hear, but not understand, / you shall indeed look, but never see. / Gross
20 is the heart of this people, / they will hardly hear with their ears, / they have closed their eyes, / lest they see with their eyes / and
· hear with their ears / and un-
25 derstand with their heart and be converted, / and I heal them.' / But blessed are your eyes, because they see, and your ears, because they hear. Amen, I say
30 to you, many prophets and righteous people longed to see what you see but did not see it, and to hear what you hear but did not hear it. (3 – 17)

35

Hear then the parable of the sower. The seed sown on the path is the one who hears the word of the kingdom without
40 understanding it, and the evil one comes and steals away what was sown in his heart. The seed

The disciple of Jesus is encouraged by way of this parable to work with his internal disposition to make it more adept and receptive to grace. A rich soil can be likened to the best possible inner disposition of a soul to be receptive to grace.

sown on rocky ground is the one
who hears the word and receives
it at once with joy. But he has
no root and lasts only for a time.
When some tribulation or per-   5
secution comes because of the
word, he immediately falls away.
The seed sown among thorns is
the one who hears the word, but
then worldly anxiety and the   10
lure of riches choke the word
and it bears no fruit. But the
seed sown on rich soil is the one
who hears the word and under-
stands it, who indeed bears fruit   15
and yields a hundred or sixty or
thirtyfold....The kingdom of
heaven may be likened to a man
who sowed good seed in his
field. While everyone was asleep   20
his enemy came and sowed
weeds all through the wheat,
and then went off. When the
crop grew and bore fruit, the
weeds appeared as well. The   25
slaves of the householder came
to him and said, 'Master, did
you not sow good seed in your
field? Where have the weeds
come from?' He answered, 'An   30
enemy has done this.' His slaves
said to him, 'Do you want us to
go and pull them up?' He replied, 'No, if you pull up the
weeds you might uproot the   35
wheat along with them. Let
them grow together until harvest; then at harvest time I will
say to the harvesters, "First col-
lect the weeds and tie them in   40
bundles for burning; but gather
the wheat into my barn."' (18 – 30)

The kingdom of heaven is like
a mustard seed that a person
took and sowed in a field. It is
the smallest of all the seeds, yet
5 when full-grown it is the largest
of plants. It becomes a large bush,
and the 'birds of the sky come and
dwell in its branches.' (31 – 32)

10   The kingdom of heaven is like
yeast that a woman took and
mixed with three measures of
wheat flour until the whole
batch was leavened. (33)

One must work at being receptive to the words of Jesus.

15

He who sows good seed is the
Son of Man; the field is the
world, the good seed the children of the kingdom. The weeds
20 are the children of the evil one,
and the enemy who sows them
is the devil. The harvest is the
end of the age, and the harvesters are angels. Just as weeds are
25 collected and burned [up] with
fire, so will it be at the end of
the age. The Son of Man will
send his angels, and they will
collect out of his kingdom all
30 who cause others to sin and all
evildoers. They will throw them
into the fiery furnace, where
there will be wailing and grinding of teeth. Then the righteous
35 will shine like the sun in the
kingdom of their Father. Whoever has ears ought to hear.
(37 – 43)

One must make an endeavor in
order to attain to the kingdom
of heaven.

40   The kingdom of heaven is like
a treasure buried in a field,
which a person finds and hides

again, and out of joy goes and sells all that he has and buys that field. (44)

Again, the kingdom of heaven is like a merchant searching for fine pearls. When he finds a pearl of great price, he goes and sells all that he has and buys it. (45)

Again, the kingdom of heaven is like a net thrown into the sea, which collects fish of every kind. When it is full they haul it ashore and sit down to put what is good into buckets. What is bad they throw away. Thus it will be at the end of the age. The angels will go out and separate the wicked from the righteous and throw them into the fiery furnace, where there will be wailing and grinding of teeth.
(47 – 50)

Then every scribe who has been instructed in the kingdom of heaven is like the head of a household who brings from his storeroom both the new and the old. (52)

Chapter 15

And why do you break the commandment of God for the sake of your tradition? For God said, 'Honor your father and your mother,' and 'Whoever curses father or mother shall die.' But you say, 'Whoever says to father or mother, "any sup-

One must exercise prudence and a bit of shrewdness to obtain salvation.

The Commandments of God do not invite rationalization.

port you might have had from
me is dedicated to God," need
not honor his father.' You have
nullified the word of God for
5 the sake of your tradition.
Hypocrites, well did Isaiah
prophesy about you when he
said: / 'This people honors me
with their lips, / but their hearts
10 are far from me; / in vain do they
worship me, / teaching as doctrines human precepts.' (3 – 9)

Hear and understand. It is not
15 what enters one's mouth that
defiles that person; but what
comes out of the mouth is what
defiles one. (10 – 11)

20 Every plant that my heavenly
Father has not planted will be
uprooted. Let them alone; they
are blind guides [of the blind].
If a blind person leads a blind
25 person, both will fall into a pit.
(13 – 14)

Do you not realize that everything that enters the mouth
30 passes into the stomach and is
expelled into the latrine? But the
things that come out of the
mouth come from the heart,
and they defile. For from the
35 heart come evil thoughts, murder, adultery, unchastity, theft,
false witness, blasphemy. These
are what defile a person, but to
eat with unwashed hands does
40 not defile. (17 – 20)

Chapter 16

[In the evening you say, 'To-morrow will be fair, for the sky is red'; and, in the morning, 'To-day will be stormy, for the sky is red and threatening.' You know how to judge the appearance of the sky, but you cannot judge the signs of the times.] An evil and unfaithful generation seeks a sign, but no sign will be given it except the sign of Jonah....Look out, and beware of the leaven of the Pharisees and Sadducees. (2 – 4)

You of little faith, why do you conclude among yourselves that it is because you have no bread? Do you not yet understand, and do you not remember the five loaves for the five thousand, and how many wicker baskets you took up? Or the seven loaves for the four thousand, and how many baskets you took up? How do you not comprehend that I was not speaking to you about bread? Beware of the leaven of the Pharisees and Sadducees.
(8 – 11)

Who do people say that the Son of Man is?...But who do you say that I am?...Blessed are you, Simon son of Jonah. For flesh and blood has not revealed this to you, but my heavenly Father. And so I say to you, you are Peter, and upon this rock I will build my church, and the gates of the netherworld shall not prevail against it. I will give

There is a personal responsibility for each person to make an evaluation on the signs of the times.

One has a personal responsibility to give recognition to Jesus as the Messiah.

you the keys to the kingdom of heaven. Whatever you bind on earth shall be bound in heaven; and whatever you loose on earth shall be loosed in heaven.

(13 – 19)

Whoever wishes to come after me must deny himself, take up his cross, and follow me. For whoever wishes to save his life will lose it, but whoever loses his life for my sake will find it.

(24 – 25)

What profit would there be for one to gain the whole world and forfeit his life? Or what can one give in exchange for his life? For the Son of Man will come with his angels in his Father's glory, and then he will repay everyone according to his conduct. Amen, I say to you, there are some standing here who will not taste death until they see the Son of Man coming in his kingdom.

(26 – 28)

Chapter 17

Elijah will indeed come and restore all things; but I tell you that Elijah has already come, and they did not recognize him but did to him whatever they pleased. So also will the Son of Man suffer at their hands.

(11 – 12)

Amen, I say to you, if you have

Whoever wishes to be a follower of Jesus must deny himself, take up his cross and follow Him. One who clings to himself loses sight of Christ; one who gives up his life for Christ, will indeed find it.

Material gains will not bring about the fulfillment of the purpose for which man has been upon the earth.

faith the size of a mustard seed, you will say to this mountain, 'Move from here to there,' and it will move. Nothing will be impossible for you. (20)

Recognize and experience the power of faith.

5

Chapter 18

Amen, I say to you, unless you turn and become like children, you will not enter the kingdom of heaven. Whoever humbles himself like this child is the greatest in the kingdom of heaven. And whoever receives one child such as this in my name receives me.

Childlike simplicity is needed as a requisite to enter into the king- 10 dom of heaven.

Humbling yourself as a little child will merit you the quality of "greatest" in the kingdom of 15 heaven.

Whoever causes one of these little ones who believe in me to sin, it would be better for him to have a great millstone hung around his neck and to be drowned in the depths of the sea. Woe to the world because of things that cause sin! Such things must come, but woe to the one through whom they come! (3 – 7)

Whatever is the source of scan- 20 dal must be rooted out vigorously.

25

If your hand or foot causes you to sin, cut it off and throw it away. It is better for you to enter into life maimed or crippled than with two hands or two feet to be thrown into eternal fire. And if your eye causes you to sin, tear it out and throw it away. It is better for you to enter into life with one eye than with two eyes to be thrown into fiery Gehenna. (8 – 9)

30

There must be a decisive battle waged against the occasions of 35 sin.

40

See that you do not despise one of these little ones, for I say to you that their angels in heaven always look upon the face of my heavenly Father. (10)

What is your opinion? If a man has a hundred sheep and one of them goes astray, will he not leave the ninety-nine in the hills and go in search of the stray? And if he finds it, amen, I say to you, he rejoices more over it than over the ninety-nine that did not stray. In just the same way, it is not the will of your heavenly Father that one of these little ones be lost.
(12 – 14)

If your brother sins [against you], go and tell him his fault between you and him alone. If he listens to you, you have won over your brother. If he does not listen, take one or two others along with you, so that 'every fact may be established on the testimony of two or three witnesses.' If he refuses to listen to them, tell the church. If he refuses to listen even to the church, then treat him as you would a Gentile or a tax collector. (15 – 17)

Amen, I say to you, whatever you bind on earth shall be bound in heaven, and whatever you loose on earth shall be loosed in heaven. (18)

Do not despise little children.

The power of forgiveness is given to the Apostles.
It comes along with the power of binding, that is, the power of authority to make laws.

Again, [amen,] I say to you, if two of you agree on earth about anything for which they are to pray, it shall be granted to them by my heavenly Father. For where two or three are gathered together in my name, there am I in the midst of them.

(19 – 20)

Herein is present the power of prayer when more than one does so. Our heavenly Father is disposed to send down blessings upon those who gather together in the name of Jesus, His Son.

I say to you, not seven times but seventy-seven times. That is why the kingdom of heaven may be likened to a king who decided to settle accounts with his servants. When he began the accounting, a debtor was brought before him who owed him a huge amount. Since he had no way of paying it back, his master ordered him to be sold, along with his wife, his children, and all his property, in payment of the debt. At that, the servant fell down, did him homage, and said, 'Be patient with me, and I will pay you back in full.' Moved with compassion the master of that servant let him go and forgave him the loan. When that servant had left, he found one of his fellow servants who owed him a much smaller amount. He seized him and started to choke him, demanding, 'Pay back what you owe.' Falling to his knees, his fellow servant begged him, 'Be patient with me, and I will pay you back.' But he refused. Instead, he had him put in prison until he paid back the debt.

Follow the process of reconciliation with your brother as presented.

When two or three gather together in prayer there are genuine blessings that come down from the loving Father.

Now when his fellow servants saw what had happened, they were deeply disturbed, and went to their master and reported the
5 whole affair. His master summoned him and said to him, 'You wicked servant! I forgave you your entire debt because you begged me to. Should you
10 not have had pity on your fellow servant, as I had pity on you?' Then in anger his master handed him over to the torturers until he should pay back the
15 whole debt. So will my heavenly Father do to you, unless each of you forgives his brother from his heart. (22 – 35)

One is always to be forgiving of those who do you harm.

20 **Chapter 19**

Have you not read that from the beginning the Creator 'made them male and female' and said,
25 'For this reason a man shall leave his father and mother and be joined to his wife, and the two shall become one flesh'? So they are no longer two, but one flesh.
30 Therefore, what God has joined together, no human being must separate....Because of the hardness of your hearts Moses allowed you to divorce your wives,
35 but from the beginning it was not so. I say to you, whoever divorces his wife (unless the marriage is unlawful) and marries another commits
40 adultery....Not all can accept [this] word, but only those to whom that is granted. Some are

"A man shall leave his father and mother and be joined to his wife, and the two shall become one flesh."

What God has joined together, no human being must separate.

Whoever divorces his wife (unless the marriage is unlawful) and marries another commits adultery.

incapable of marriage because they were born so; some, because they were made so by others; some, because they have renounced marriage for the sake of the kingdom of heaven. Whoever can accept this ought to accept it. (4 – 12)

Let the children come to me, and do not prevent them; for the kingdom of heaven belongs to such as these. (14)

Why do you ask me about the good? There is only One who is good. If you wish to enter into life, keep the commandments. (17)

'You shall not kill; you shall not commit adultery; you shall not steal; you shall not bear false witness; honor your father and your mother'; and 'you shall love your neighbor as yourself.' (18 – 19)

If you wish to be perfect, go, sell what you have and give to [the] poor, and you will have treasure in heaven. Then come, follow me. (21)

Amen, I say to you, it will be hard for one who is rich to enter the kingdom of heaven. Again I say to you, it is easier for a camel to pass through the eye of a needle than for one who is rich to enter the kingdom of God. (23 – 24)

5

"Let children come to me and 10 do not prevent them from the kingdom."

15

20

'You shall not kill; you shall not commit adultery; you shall not steal; you shall not bear false witness; honor your father and your mother'; and 'you shall love 25 your neighbor as yourself.'

Detachment from the things of the world must be made before 30 one can possibly make a commitment to follow Jesus.

The Lord speaks of those who 35 are attached to their riches and do not see them as coming forth from a loving Father.

40

When the disciples heard this, they were greatly astonished and said, "Who then can be saved?" ...For human beings this is im-
5 possible, but for God all things are possible. (26)

Grace comes to those who have riches if they give recognition to the One Who is the source of all riches, both material and spiritual.

Amen, I say to you that you who have followed me, in the
10 new age, when the Son of Man is seated on his throne of glory, will yourselves sit on twelve thrones, judging the twelve tribes of Israel. And everyone
15 who has given up houses or brothers or sisters or father or mother or children or lands for the sake of my name will receive a hundred times more, and will
20 inherit eternal life. But many who are first will be last, and the last will be first. (28 – 30)

Note: "In the new age - - - :

To be great in the kingdom, one must be a servant to others.

Chapter 20

25
The kingdom of heaven is like a landowner who went out at dawn to hire laborers for his vineyard. After agreeing with
30 them for the usual daily wage, he sent them into his vineyard. Going out about nine o'clock, he saw others standing idle in the marketplace, and he said to
35 them, 'You too go into my vine-yard, and I will give you what is just.' So they went off. [And] he went out again around noon, and around three o'clock, and
40 did likewise. Going out about five o'clock, he found others standing around, and said to

them, 'Why do you stand here idle all day?' They answered, 'Because no one has hired us.' He said to them, 'You too go into my vineyard.' When it was evening the owner of the vine-yard said to his foreman, 'Sum-mon the laborers and give them their pay, beginning with the last and ending with the first.' When those who had started about five o'clock came, each received the usual daily wage. So when the first came, they thought that they would receive more, but each of them also got the usual wage. And on receiv-ing it they grumbled against the landowner, saying, 'These last ones worked only one hour, and you have made them equal to us, who bore the day's burden and the heat.' He said to one of them in reply, 'My friend, I am not cheating you. Did you not agree with me for the usual daily wage? Take what is yours and go. What if I wish to give this last one the same as you? [Or] am I not free to do as I wish with my own money? Are you envi-ous because I am generous?' Thus, the last will be first, and the first will be last. (1 – 16)

Behold, we are going up to Jerusalem, and the Son of Man will be handed over to the chief priests and the scribes, and they will condemn him to death, and hand him over to the Gentiles to be mocked and scourged and

God is the God of justice and of mercy. He gives to those who deserve, and He also gives that which is beyond what one de-serves.

crucified, and he will be raised on the third day. (18 – 19)

You know that the rulers of
5 the Gentiles lord it over them, and the great ones make their authority over them felt. But it shall not be so among you. Rather, whoever wishes to be
10 great among you shall be your servant; whoever wishes to be first among you shall be your slave. Just so, the Son of Man did not come to be served but
15 to serve and to give his life as a ransom for many. (25 – 28)

Lording it over others is not what the followers of Jesus are to do. Instead, they are to feel honored that they could be of assistance to those who are in need.

Chapter 21

20 Amen, I say to you, if you have faith and do not waver, not only will you do what has been done to the fig tree, but even if you say to this mountain, 'Be lifted
25 up and thrown into the sea,' it will be done. Whatever you ask for in prayer with faith, you will receive. (21 - 22)

Have faith and do not waver.

30 A man had two sons. He came to the first and said, 'Son, go out and work in the vineyard today.' He said in reply, 'I will not,' but afterwards he changed his mind
35 and went. The man came to the other son and gave the same order. He said in reply, 'Yes, sir,' but did not go. Which of the two did his father's
40 will?…Amen, I say to you, tax collectors and prostitutes are entering the kingdom of God

Everyone benefits when they respond to grace. A grace is an illumination of the mind plus an inspiration of the will that comes from God in favor of helping the recipient to accomplish something that is pleasing to Him.

before you. When John came to you in the way of righteousness, you did not believe him; but tax collectors and prostitutes did. Yet even when you saw that, you did not later change your minds and believe him. (28 – 32)

Hear another parable. There was a landowner who planted a vineyard, put a hedge around it, dug a wine press in it, and built a tower. Then he leased it to tenants and went on a journey. When vintage time drew near, he sent his servants to the tenants to obtain his produce. But the tenants seized the servants and one they beat, another they killed, and a third they stoned. Again he sent other servants, more numerous than the first ones, but they treated them in the same way. Finally, he sent his son to them, thinking, 'They will respect my son.' But when the tenants saw the son, they said to one another, 'This is the heir. Come, let us kill him and acquire his inheritance.' They seized him, threw him out of the vineyard, and killed him. What will the owner of the vineyard do to those tenants when he comes? (33 – 40)

Did you never read in the scriptures: / 'The stone that the builders rejected / has become the cornerstone; / by the Lord has this been done, / and it is wonderful in our eyes?' / There-

fore, I say to you, the kingdom
of God will be taken away from
you and given to a people that
will produce its fruit. [The one
5 who falls on this stone will be
dashed to pieces; and it will
crush anyone on whom it falls.]
(42 – 44)

Producing fruit and the kingdom of God are related.

10 **Chapter 22**

The kingdom of heaven may
be likened to a king who gave a
wedding feast for his son. He
15 dispatched his servants to sum-
mon the invited guests to the
feast, but they refused to come.
A second time he sent other servants, saying, 'Tell those invited:
20 "Behold, I have prepared my
banquet, my calves and fattened
cattle are killed, and everything
is ready; come to the feast."
Some ignored the invitation and
25 went away, one to his farm, another to his business. The rest
laid hold of his servants, mis-
treated them, and killed them.
The king was enraged and sent
30 his troops, destroyed those mur-
derers, and burned their city.
Then he said to his servants,
'The feast is ready, but those
who were invited were not wor-
35 thy to come. Go out, therefore,
into the main roads and invite
to the feast whomever you find.'
The servants went out into the
streets and gathered all they
40 found, bad and good alike, and
the hall was filled with guests.
But when the king came in to

Be one of those who allow
themselves to be chosen.

meet the guests he saw a man there not dressed in a wedding garment. He said to him, 'My friend, how is it that you came in here without a wedding garment?' But he was reduced to silence. Then the king said to his attendants, 'Bind his hands and feet, and cast him into the darkness outside, where there will be wailing and grinding of teeth.' Many are invited, but few are chosen. (2 – 14)

Then repay to Caesar what belongs to Caesar and to God what belongs to God. (21)

Give to God what belongs to Him and to the government what belongs to the government.

At the resurrection they neither marry nor are given in marriage but are like the angels in heaven. And concerning the resurrection of the dead, have you not read what was said to you by God, 'I am the God of Abraham, the God of Isaac, and the God of Jacob?' He is not the God of the dead but of the living. (30 – 32)

You shall love the Lord, your God, with all your heart, with all your soul, and with all your mind. This is the greatest and the first commandment. The second is like it: You shall love your neighbor as yourself. The whole law and the prophets depend on these two commandments. (37 – 40)

You shall love the Lord, your God, with all your heart, with all your soul, and with all your mind. This is the greatest and the first commandment. The second is like it: You shall love your neighbor as yourself. The whole law and the prophets depend on these two commandments.

Chapter 23

The scribes and the Pharisees have taken their seat on the chair of Moses. Therefore, do and observe all things whatsoever
5 they tell you, but do not follow their example. For they preach but they do not practice. They tie up heavy burdens [hard to carry] and lay them on people's
10 shoulders, but they will not lift a finger to move them. All their works are performed to be seen. They widen their phylacteries and lengthen their tassels. They
15 love places of honor at banquets, seats of honor in synagogues, greetings in marketplaces, and the salutation 'Rabbi.' As for you, do not be called 'Rabbi.'
20 You have but one teacher, and you are all brothers. Call no one on earth your father; you have but one Father in heaven. Do not be called 'Master'; you have
25 but one master, the Messiah. The greatest among you must be your servant. Whoever exalts himself will be humbled; but whoever humbles himself will
30 be exalted. (2 – 12)

Act contrary to the way the Pharisees did: do not perform works just to be seen, do not look for places of honor. The source of your life is the Father. Jesus is to be first in all that you do, in all of your life.

Do not exalt yourself; humble yourself.

Woe to you, scribes and Pharisees, you hypocrites. You lock the kingdom of heaven before
35 human beings. You do not enter yourselves, nor do you allow entrance to those trying to enter. (13)

Do not be concerned about appearances, but work with your internal attitudes and dispositions.

40 Woe to you, scribes and Pharisees, you hypocrites. You traverse sea and land to make one con-

Be not a hypocrite; Let the virtue of your soul work its way through to your external behavior.

vert, and when that happens you make him a child of Gehenna twice as much as yourselves. (15)

Woe to you, blind guides, who say, 'If one swears by the temple, it means nothing, but if one swears by the gold of the temple, one is obligated.' Blind fools, which is greater, the gold, or the temple that made the gold sacred? And you say, 'If one swears by the altar, it means nothing, but if one swears by the gift on the altar, one is obligated.' You blind ones, which is greater, the gift, or the altar that makes the gift sacred? One who swears by the altar swears by it and all that is upon it; one who swears by the temple swears by it and by him who dwells in it; one who swears by heaven swears by the throne of God and by him who is seated on it. (16 – 22)

Woe to you, scribes and Pharisees, you hypocrites. You pay tithes of mint and dill and cummin, and have neglected the weightier things of the law: judgment and mercy and fidelity. [But] these you should have done, without neglecting the others. Blind guides, who strain out the gnat and swallow the camel! (23 – 24)

Woe to you, scribes and Pharisees, you hypocrites. You cleanse the outside of cup and dish, but inside they are full of plunder

Jesus exposes the hypocrisy of the Pharisees and points out to them their faults. He lets them know how wrong they are and

and self-indulgence. Blind Pharisee; cleanse first the inside of the cup, so that the outside also may be clean. (25 – 26)

Woe to you, scribes and Pharisees, you hypocrites. You are like whitewashed tombs, which appear beautiful on the outside, but inside are full of dead men's bones and every kind of filth. Even so, on the outside you appear righteous, but inside you are filled with hypocrisy and evildoing. (27 – 28)

Woe to you, scribes and Pharisees, you hypocrites. You build the tombs of the prophets and adorn the memorials of the righteous, and you say, 'If we had lived in the days of our ancestors, we would not have joined them in shedding the prophets' blood.' Thus you bear witness against yourselves that you are the children of those who murdered the prophets; now fill up what your ancestors measured out! You serpents, you brood of vipers, how can you flee from the judgment of Gehenna? Therefore, behold, I send to you prophets and wise men and scribes; some of them you will kill and crucify, some of them you will scourge in your synagogues and pursue from town to town, so that there may come upon you all the righteous blood shed upon earth, from the righteous blood of Abel to the blood

that they are the leaders of the people and still are leading them astray.

"You serpents, you brood of vipers," are strong words. In all of these "Woes", Jesus goes forward with conviction and with truth, still in His love for both the scribes and the Pharisees, but also in love with His people. He takes the side of the people because the are suffering at the hands of those who should be of help to them instead.

of Zechariah, the son of Barachiah, whom you murdered between the sanctuary and the altar. Amen, I say to you, all these things will come upon this generation. (29 – 36)

Jerusalem, Jerusalem, you who kill the prophets and stone those sent to you, how many times I yearned to gather your children together, as a hen gathers her young under her wings, but you were unwilling! Behold, your house will be abandoned, desolate. I tell you, you will not see me again until you say, 'Blessed is he who comes in the name of the Lord.' (37 – 39)

Chapter 24

You see all these things, do you not? Amen, I say to you, there will not be left here a stone upon another stone that will not be thrown down.…See that no one deceives you. For many will come in my name, saying, 'I am the Messiah,' and they will deceive many. You will hear of wars and reports of wars; see that you are not alarmed, for these things must happen, but it will not yet be the end. Nation will rise against nation, and kingdom against kingdom; there will be famines and earthquakes from place to place. All these are the beginning of the labor pains. Then they will hand you over

Rid yourself of your own faults and sins before you go out to take authority over another's behavior.

5

10

Be willing to let Jesus take you under His care.

15

20

25

30

35

40

to persecution, and they will kill you. You will be hated by all nations because of my name. And then many will be led into
5 sin; they will betray and hate one another. Many false prophets will arise and deceive many; and because of the increase of evildoing, the love of many will
10 grow cold. But the one who perseveres to the end will be saved. And this gospel of the kingdom will be preached throughout the world as a witness to all nations,
15 and then the end will come.

(2 – 14)

Do not permit yourself to be deceived by others.

When you see the desolating abomination spoken of through
20 Daniel the prophet standing in the holy place (let the reader understand), then those in Judea must flee to the mountains, a person on the housetop must
25 not go down to get things out of his house, a person in the field must not return to get his cloak. Woe to pregnant women and nursing mothers in those days.
30 Pray that your flight not be in winter or on the sabbath, for at that time there will be great tribulation, such as has not been since the beginning of the world
35 until now, nor ever will be. And if those days had not been shortened, no one would be saved; but for the sake of the elect they will be shortened. If anyone says
40 to you then, 'Look, here is the Messiah!' or, 'There he is!' do not believe it. False messiahs and

Take a responsibility to check the signs of the times.

Do know that there will be a time when disciples of the end times will have to flee into the mountains or wherever safety is being offered.

false prophets will arise, and they will perform signs and wonders so great as to deceive, if that were possible, even the elect. Behold, I have told it to you beforehand. So if they say to you, 'He is in the desert,' do not go out there; if they say, 'He is in the inner rooms,' do not believe it. For just as lightning comes from the east and is seen as far as the west, so will the coming of the Son of Man be. Wherever the corpse is, there the vultures will gather.

Immediately after the tribulation of those days, / the sun will be darkened, / and the moon will not give its light, / and the stars will fall from the sky, / and the powers of the heavens will be shaken. / And then the sign of the Son of Man will appear in heaven, and all the tribes of the earth will mourn, and they will see the Son of Man coming upon the clouds of heaven with power and great glory. And he will send out his angels with a trumpet blast, and they will gather his elect from the four winds, from one end of the heavens to the other.

Learn a lesson from the fig tree. When its branch becomes tender and sprouts leaves, you know that summer is near. In the same way, when you see all these things, know that he is near, at the gates. Amen, I say to you, this generation will not pass away until all these things

Do not let your love grow cold. Persevere in your faith and in your good deeds.

have taken place. Heaven and earth will pass away, but my words will not pass away.

(15 – 35)

5

But of that day and hour no one knows, neither the angels of heaven, nor the Son, but the Father alone. For as it was in the 10 days of Noah, so it will be at the coming of the Son of Man. In [those] days before the flood, they were eating and drinking, marrying and giving in mar-15 riage, up to the day that Noah entered the ark. They did not know until the flood came and carried them all away. So will it be [also] at the coming of the 20 Son of Man. Two men will be out in the field; one will be taken, and one will be left. Two women will be grinding at the mill; one will be taken, and one 25 will be left. Therefore, stay awake! For you do not know on which day your Lord will come. Be sure of this: if the master of the house had known the hour 30 of night when the thief was coming, he would have stayed awake and not let his house be broken into. So too, you must also be prepared for at an hour 35 you do not expect, the Son of Man will come. (36 – 44)

Who, then, is the faithful and prudent servant, whom the 40 Master has put in charge of his household to distribute to them their food at the proper time?

Be alerted that there will come a time when fleeing will be necessary. A time will come when absolute urgency will be required.

Prayer can alter conditions in the end times.

Be alerted that there will be a time when many will be led astray by deception, to the degree of performing wonders to trap others into following them, thus abandoning truth. The chosen few will be targeted.

Be prepared for what is to come. These things will surely come about by Jesus' own promise.

Stay awake! This is serious matter. There is on its way a "red alert". Though there is the fact of this, the exact time as to when is up to the Father. Nonetheless,

Blessed is the servant whom his master on his arrival finds doing so. Amen, I say to you, he will put him in charge of all his property. But if that wicked servant says to himself, 'My master is long delayed, and begins to beat his fellow servants, and eat and drink with drunkards, the servant's master will come on an unexpected day and at an unknown hour and will punish him severely and assign him a place with the hypocrites, where there will be wailing and grinding of teeth. (45 – 51)

Chapter 25

Then the kingdom of heaven will be like ten virgins who took their lamps and went out to meet the bridegroom. Five of them were foolish and five were wise. The foolish ones, when taking their lamps, brought no oil with them, but the wise brought flasks of oil with their lamps. Since the bridegroom was long delayed, they all became drowsy and fell asleep. At midnight, there was a cry, 'Behold, the bridegroom! Come out to meet him!' Then all those virgins got up and trimmed their lamps. The foolish ones said to the wise, 'Give us some of your oil, for our lamps are going out.' But the wise ones replied, 'No, for there may not be enough for us and you. Go instead to the merchants and

to know of the fact of these happenings is one thing, to be prepared for them is of the essence.

5

10

15

Charity has its limits. Be prepared for the unexpected. It can come when one least expects it. 20

25

30

35

The responsibility of providing for oneself is of the utmost importance. One is not to count on others. 40

buy some for yourselves.' While they went off to buy it, the bridegroom came and those who were ready went into the
5 wedding feast with him. Then the door was locked. Afterwards the other virgins came and said, 'Lord, Lord, open the door for us!' But he said in reply, 'Amen,
10 I say to you, I do not know you.' Therefore, stay awake, for you know neither the day nor the hour. (1 – 13)

15   It will be as when a man who was going on journey called in his servants and entrusted his possessions to them. To one he gave five talents; to another, two;
20 to a third, one -- to each according to his ability. Then he went away. Immediately the one who received five talents went and traded with them, and made
25 another five. Likewise, the one who received two made another two. But the man who received one went off and dug a hole in the ground and buried his
30 master's money. After a long time the master of those servants came back and settled accounts with them. The one who had received five talents came for-
35 ward bringing the additional five. He said, 'Master, you gave me five talents. See, I have made five more.' His master said to him, 'Well done, my good and
40 faithful servant. Since you were faithful in small matters, I will give you great responsibilities.

The Master gives His listeners a long dissertation giving a descriptive explanation of just how it is going to be at the end, at a time when He will call all into a certain place and straighten all of the records of life. The good will be rewarded, the evil will be punished.

Come, share your master's joy.'
[Then] the one who had received two talents also came forward and said, 'Master, you gave
me two talents. See, I have made   5
two more.' His master said to
him, 'Well done, my good and
faithful servant. Since you were
faithful in small matters, I will
give you great responsibilities.   10
Come, share your master's joy.'
Then the one who had received
the one talent came forward and
said, 'Master, I knew you were a
demanding person, harvesting   15
where you did not plant and
gathering where you did not
scatter; so out of fear I went off
and buried your talent in the
ground. Here it is back.' His   20
master said to him in reply, 'You
wicked, lazy servant! So you
knew that I harvest where I did
not plant and gather where I did
not scatter? Should you not then   25
have put my money in the bank
so that I could have got it back
with interest on my return? Now
then! Take the talent from him
and give it to the one with ten.   30
For to everyone who has, more
will be given and he will grow
rich; but from the one who has   A time of reckoning is ap-
not, even what he has will be   proaching for each person. Ul-
taken away. And throw this use-   timately everyone is on his own   35
less servant into the darkness   and must take responsibility for
outside, where there will be   one's decisions and behavior.
wailing and grinding of teeth.'
                        (14– 30)

When the Son of Man comes
in his glory, and all the angels   40

with him, he will sit upon his glorious throne, and all the nations will be assembled before him. And he will separate them
5 one from another, as a shepherd separates the sheep from the goats. He will place the sheep on his right and the goats on his left. Then the king will say to
10 those on his right, 'Come, you who are blessed by my Father. Inherit the kingdom prepared for you from the foundation of the world.' (31 – 34)
15

'For I was hungry and you gave me food, I was thirsty and you gave me drink, a stranger and you welcomed me, naked
20 and you clothed me, ill and you cared for me, in prison and you visited me.' Then the righteous will answer him and say, 'Lord. when did we see you hungry and
25 feed you, or thirsty and give you drink? When did we see you a stranger and welcome you, or naked and clothe you? When did we see you ill or in prison,
30 and visit you?' And the king will say to them in reply, 'Amen, I say to you, whatever you did for one of these least brothers of mine, you did for me.' Then he
35 will say to those on his left, 'Depart from me, you accursed, into the eternal fire prepared for the devil and his angels. For I was hungry and you gave me no
40 food, I was thirsty and you gave me no drink, a stranger and you gave me no welcome, naked and

Loving service to one's fellow man will be eternally rewarded; lack of loving service to one's fellow man will be punished.

you gave me no clothing, ill and in prison, and you did not care for me.' Then they will answer and say, 'Lord, when did we see you hungry or thirsty or a stranger or naked or ill or in prison, and not minister to your needs?' He will answer them, 'Amen, I say to you, what you did not do for one of these least ones, you did not do for me.' And these will go off to eternal punishment, but the righteous to eternal life. (35 – 46)

Chapter 26

Take and eat; this is my body....Drink from it, all of you, for this is my blood of the covenant, which will be shed on behalf of many for the forgiveness of sins. I tell you; from now on I shall not drink this fruit of the vine until the day when I drink it with you new in the kingdom of my Father.

(26 – 29)

It was at the Last Supper, the night before Jesus died that He established the Sacrament of the Eucharist. He gave His Apostles the command that they were to do as He did. The Sacrifice of the Mass is what has, down through the centuries wherein, in a mystical manner, the act that was started at the Last Supper continues.

Watch and pray that you may not undergo the test. The spirit is willing, but the flesh is weak.

(41)

Put your sword back into its sheath, for all who take the sword will perish by the sword.

(52)

Chapter 28

All power in heaven and on

Make disciples of all nations.

earth has been given to me. Go, therefore, and make disciples of all nations, baptizing them in the name of the Father, and of the Son, and of the holy Spirit, teaching them to observe all that I have commanded you. And behold, I am with you always, until the end of the age.

(18 – 20)

This is the command that Jesus gave to His Apostles, commissioning them to preach what He had taught them and to baptize those who believed in Him. It is at this happening that the Holy Spirit takes up His abode within the soul.

Notes

Notes

Searching Through the Teachings of Jesus - ~ ~

As Found in the Gospel of St. Mark

So as to Implant Them
into Your Heart

Chapter 2

But that you may know that the Son of Man has authority
5 to forgive sins on earth -- ...I say to you, rise, pick up your mat, and go home. (10 – 11)

Sin is a transgression against God. Jesus is the Second Person of the Blessed Trinity, as much God as is the Father and the Spirit. He has the absolute right to forgive sins.

Those who are well do not
10 need a physician, but the sick do. I did not come to call the righteous but sinners." (17)

Jesus does not change. What He says here applies to each person on earth living in whatever century.

Can the wedding guests fast
15 while the bridegroom is with them? As long as they have the bridegroom with them they cannot fast. But the days will come when the bridegroom is
20 taken away from them, and then they will fast on that day. No one sews a piece of unshrunken cloth on an old cloak. If he does, its fullness pulls away, the new
25 from the old, and the tear gets worse. Likewise, no one pours new wine into old wineskins. Otherwise, the wine will burst the skins, and both the wine and
30 the skins are ruined. Rather, new wine is poured into fresh wineskins. (19 – 22)

Jesus knew well that He could not expect too much from the Apostles at the time when He was teaching so many new things. He was an expert teacher and He knew that in time they would be able to fast.

Have you never read what
35 David did when he was in need and he and his companions were hungry? How he went into the house of God when Abiathar was high priest and ate the bread
40 of offering that only the priests could lawfully eat, and shared it with his companions?...The

The leaders of the people were badgering Jesus. This time it was with regard to what was allowed for the disciples to do on the Sabbath. Very wisely He reminded these leaders that He, as the Son of God, was entitled to make an exception. He reminded them of what David did

sabbath was made for man, not man for the sabbath. That is why the Son of Man is lord even of the sabbath. (25 – 28)

Chapter 6

A prophet is not without honor except in his native place and among his own kin and in his own house. (4)

Wherever you enter a house, stay there until you leave from there. Whatever place does not welcome you or listen to you, leave there and shake the dust off your feet in testimony against them. (10 – 11)

Come away by yourselves to a deserted place and rest a while. (31)

Take courage, it is I, do not be afraid! (50)

Chapter 7

Well did Isaiah prophesy about you hypocrites, as it is written: / 'This people honors me with their lips, / but their hearts are far from me; / In vain do they worship me, / teaching as doctrines human precepts.' / You disregard God's commandment but cling to human tradition. How well you have set aside the commandment of God in order to uphold your tradition! For Moses said, 'Honor

when a similar situation existed.

What Jesus is saying is that a prophet is given recognition by everyone except by his own family and relatives.

The followers of Jesus should never force His teaching on anyone. If there are those who choose not to listen, one should desist from putting forth any pressure.

As this was good advice to the Apostles, it is good advice for Jesus' followers.

In all hardships, Jesus is alongside.

What Jesus chides the leaders of the chosen people about, He would do the same today. There are those in our midst who put others under pressure to observe mere human laws and themselves do nothing to promote the laws of God.

your father and your mother,'
and 'Whoever curses father or
mother shall die.' Yet you say,
'If a person says to father or
5 mother, "Any support you
might have had from me is
orban"' (meaning, dedicated to
God), you allow him to do
nothing more for his father or
10 mother. You nullify the word
of God in favor of your tradition that you have handed on.
And you do many such
things....Hear me, all of you,
15 and understand. Nothing that
enters one from outside can defile that person; but the things
that come out from within are
what defile. (6 – 15)

20

Are even you likewise without
understanding? Do you not realize that everything that goes
into a person from outside can-
25 not defile, since it enters not the
heart but the stomach and passes
out into the latrine?...But what
comes out of a person, that is
what defiles. From within
30 people, from their hearts, come
evil thoughts, unchastity, theft,
murder, adultery, greed, malice,
deceit, licentiousness, envy, blasphemy, arrogance, folly. All
35 these evils come from within
and they defile. (18 – 23)

Chapter 8

40 Watch out, guard against the
leaven of the Pharisees and the
leaven of Herod. (15)

Real defilement of a person is
the evil that comes out from
within himself such as those
here listed by Jesus.

Do not allow yourself to be in-
fluenced by the people of pride.

Whoever wishes to come after me must deny himself, take up his cross, and follow me. For whoever wishes to save his life will lose it, but whoever loses his life for my sake and that of the gospel will save it. What profit is there for one to gain the whole world and forfeit his life? What could one give in exchange for his life? Whoever is ashamed of me and of my words in this faithless and sinful generation, the Son of Man will be ashamed of when he comes in his Father's glory with the holy angels. (34 – 38)

The cross must be part and parcel of the life of the follower of Jesus. The hardships of everyday life keep the soul humble and humility is the ticket to heaven. 5

One's aspiration are not to be for a successful worldly life.
10

For anyone to be ashamed to speak of, and to live by, the teachings of Jesus will not merit for oneself the favorableness of 15 Jesus.

Chapter 9

20

Everything is possible to one who has faith. (23)

Faith will open wide the doors of blessings.

This kind can only come out through prayer. (29)

The power of Satan is broken through prayer. 25

If anyone wishes to be first, he shall be the last of all and the servant of all. Whoever receives one child such as this in my name, receives me; and whoever receives me, receives not me but the One who sent me. (35 – 37)

By living a life of loving service to those in need, one will receive just acclaim.
30

The acceptance of a child in Jesus' name will be as accepting Jesus and the Father.

Do not prevent him. There is no one who performs a mighty deed in my name who can at the same time speak ill of me. For whoever is not against us is for us. Anyone who gives you a cup of water to drink because you belong to Christ, amen, I say to

People who perform mighty 35 deeds in the name of Jesus ought not to be looked upon as being outside of the fold. Anyone who does not oppose Jesus is on His side. Anyone who gives service 40 to one of the fold will surely be rewarded.

you, will surely not lose his reward. (39 – 41)

Whoever causes one of these
little ones who believe [in me]
to sin, it would be better for him
if a great millstone were put
around his neck and he were
thrown into the sea. If your
hand causes you to sin, cut it off.
It is better for you to enter into
life maimed than with two
hands to go into Gehenna, into
the unquenchable fire. And if
your foot causes you to sin, cut
it off. It is better for you to enter into life crippled than with
two feet to be thrown into
Gehenna. And if your eye causes
you to sin, pluck it out. Better
for you to enter into the kingdom of God with one eye than
with two eyes to be thrown into
Gehenna, where 'their worm
does not die, and the fire is not
quenched.'
Everyone will be salted with
fire. Salt is good, but if salt becomes insipid, with what will
you restore its flavor? Keep salt
in yourselves and you will have
peace with one another.
(42 – 50)

Whoever leads a childlike believer into sin, would be better
for him were he to be put to a
violent death.

The follower of Jesus must be
ruthless in doing away with any
and all occasions of sin.

One must work for integrity in
life. Doing this will invite harmony between himself and others.

Chapter 10

Because of the hardness of your
hearts he wrote you this commandment. But from the beginning of creation, 'God made them
male and female. For this reason
a man shall leave his father

Jesus confirms the sacredness of
matrimony and insists that
those joined are as one body.
There ceases in the bond of
marriage the preeminence of
parental authority in the lives of

and mother [and be joined to his wife], and the two shall become one flesh.' So they are no longer two but one flesh. Therefore what God has joined together, no human being must separate....Whoever divorces his wife and marries another commits adultery against her; and if she divorces her husband and marries another, she commits adultery. (5 – 12)

those bonded.

Every marriage is bonded by God Himself and may not be dissolved by human authority. 5

In this joining there is to be permanence. If either one or both after a divorce marry others, all involved commit the sin of adultery. 10

Let the children come to me; do not prevent them, for the kingdom of God belongs to such as these. Amen, I say to you, whoever does not accept the kingdom of God like a child will not enter it. (14 - 15)

Childlikeness in its simplicity is what the follower of Jesus must 15 aspire to. It is the key to living the fullness of life offered by Jesus.

20

Why do you call me good? No one is good but God alone. You know the commandments: 'You shall not kill; you shall not commit adultery; you shall not steal; you shall not bear false witness; you shall not defraud; honor your father and your mother.' (18 - 19)

There are these two options 25 Jesus offers; 1) to live by the commandments, 2) total detachment in favor of a total commitment to Jesus.

30

You are lacking in one thing. Go, sell what you have, and give to [the] poor and you will have treasure in heaven; then come, follow me. (21)

35

How hard it is for those who have wealth to enter the kingdom of God!...Children, how hard it is to enter the kingdom of God! It is easier for a camel

Attachment to wealth hinders one from being a true disciple of Jesus. Grace to live a life ac- 40 cording to the teachings of Jesus is possible to the wealthy per-

to pass through [the] eye of [a] needle than for one who is rich to enter the kingdom of God.... For human beings it is impos-
5 sible, but not for God. All things are possible for God. (23 – 27)

Amen, I say to you, there is no one who has given up house
10 or brothers or sisters or mother or father or children or lands for my sake and for the sake of the gospel who will not receive a hundred times more now in this
15 present age: houses and brothers and sisters and mothers and children and lands, with persecutions, and eternal life in the age to come. But many that are
20 first will be last, and [the] last will be first. (29 – 31)

You do not know what you are asking. Can you drink the cup
25 that I drink or be baptized with the baptism with which I am baptized?...The cup that I drink, you will drink, and with the baptism with which I am
30 baptized, you will be baptized; but to sit at my right or at my left is not mine to give but is for those for whom it has been prepared. (38 – 40)

35

You know that those who are recognized as rulers over the Gentiles lord it over them, and their great ones make their au-
40 thority over them felt. But it shall not be so among you. Rather, whoever wishes to be

son, if he is disposed to God's grace and deals with his wealth as a means to an end instead of it being an end in itself.

Anyone who truly and generously gives his life over to Jesus and puts Him first in all things, will receive in return much, much more than he has given up, not only here in the present age, but also in the age to come.

The apportioning of graces and the places of glory in eternal life is to be left to the Father. The disciple of Jesus is to follow Him and leave the final reward of his loyalty to Christ to the Father.

Jesus gives Himself as the example of how His disciples are to behave. They are not to be

great among you will be your servant; whoever wishes to be first among you will be the slave of all. For the Son of Man did not come to be served but to serve and to give his life as a ransom for many. (42 – 45)

Chapter 11

Have faith in God. Amen, I say to you, whoever says to this mountain, 'Be lifted up and thrown into the sea,' and does not doubt in his heart but believes that what he says will happen, it shall be done for him. Therefore I tell you, all that you ask for in prayer, believe that you will receive it and it shall be yours. When you stand to pray, forgive anyone against whom you have a grievance, so that your heavenly Father may in turn forgive you your transgressions. (22 – 25)

Chapter 12

A man planted a vineyard, put a hedge around it, dug a wine press, and built a tower. Then he leased it to tenant farmers and left on a journey. At the proper time he sent a servant to the tenants to obtain from them some of the produce of the vineyard. But they seized him, beat him, and sent him away empty-handed. Again he sent them another servant. And that one they beat over the head and

overbearing, but they are to live in a humble state giving of themselves to those who have needs even to the extent of giving up their lives.

5

10

Have faith in God to the degree that when you truly believe that He will grant you an answer to your prayer, it will be done to you.

15

20

In prayer there must be a forgiveness to all who have done you harm. In this way you will receive forgiveness from your heavenly Father for your own transgressions.

25

30

35

40

treated shamefully. He sent yet another whom they killed. So, too, many others; some they beat, others they killed. He had
5 one other to send, a beloved son. He sent him to them last of all, thinking, 'They will respect my son.' But those tenants said to one another, 'This is the heir.
10 Come, let us kill him, and the inheritance will be ours.' So they seized him and killed him, and threw him out of the vineyard. What [then] will the owner of
15 the vineyard do? He will come, put the tenants to death, and give the vineyard to others. Have you not read this scripture passage: / 'The stone that the
20 builders rejected / has become the cornerstone; / by the Lord has this been done, / and it is wonderful in our eyes?' (1 – 11)

This parable has reference to Jesus Himself. He has come to offer salvation to His people, but because of His rejection by them, He will offer salvation to others. He is speaking primarily to the leaders of the people.

25 Repay to Caesar what belongs to Caesar and to God what belongs to God. (17)

This is the solution to the relationship of the State to the Church. Each has its proper due.

Are you not misled because
30 you do not know the scriptures or the power of God? When they rise from the dead, they neither marry nor are given in marriage, but they are like the
35 angels in heaven. As for the dead being raised, have you not read in the Book of Moses, in the passage about the bush, how God told him, 'I am the God of
40 Abraham, [the] God of Isaac, and [the] God of Jacob?' He is not God of the dead but of the

Jesus chides the leaders for their ignorance as to how things will be in the next life. He makes it clear that there will be no marriage in heaven. God is not the God of the dead, but of the living. The separation of the soul from the body in death as we know it, had never been a part of the original plan. Death as we know it, came in through Original Sin.

living. You are greatly misled.
(24 – 27)

The first is this: 'Hear, O Israel! The Lord our God is Lord alone! You shall love the Lord your God with all your heart, with all your soul, with all your mind, and with all your strength.' The second is this: 'You shall love your neighbor as yourself.' There is no other commandment greater than these.
(29 – 31)

The Ten Commandments are brought down to the Two Great Commandments by Jesus. We are to love God with our whole being and love our neighbor as ourselves. These are the fulfillment of the law and the prophets.

Beware of the scribes, who like to go around in long robes and accept greetings in the marketplaces, seats of honor in synagogues, and places of honor at banquets. They devour the houses of widows and, as a pretext, recite lengthy prayers. They will receive a very severe condemnation. (38 – 40)

In dealing with others, the follower of Jesus must be discerning. In these few verses, He gives a warning against those who take advantage of others.

Amen, I say to you, this poor widow put in more than all the other contributors to the treasury. For they have all contributed from their surplus wealth, but she, from her poverty, has contributed all she had, her whole livelihood. (43 – 44)

The disciple of Jesus takes the lesson here of giving the Lord by way of one's means rather than giving to Him directly or to those in need by way of one's surplus.

Chapter 13

See that no one deceives you. Many will come in my name saying, 'I am he,' and they will deceive many. When you hear of wars and reports of wars do

Deception is the way of Satan. Satan is the prince of the world. To live each day in a childlike manner will invite the light of the Spirit.

not be alarmed; such things must happen, but it will not yet be the end. (5 - 7)

5   Nation will rise against nation and kingdom against kingdom. There will be earthquakes from place to place and there will be famines. These are the begin-
10 nings of the labor pains.

These are some of the signs that will indicate to the disciple the general time and manner of Jesus' glorious return.

Watch out for yourselves. They will hand you over to the courts. You will be beaten in synagogues. You will be ar-
15 raigned before governors and kings because of me, as a witness before them. But the gospel must first be preached to all nations. When they lead you
20 away and hand you over, do not worry beforehand about what you are to say. But say whatever will be given to you at that hour. For it will not be you who are
25 speaking, but the holy Spirit.
(8-11)

Persecution on a grand scale will be the lot of the followers of Jesus. The sentence, "Watch out for yourselves," points out that the followers of Jesus may make an effort towards safety and survival.

It is essential that the disciple of Christ of the present day enter into a true relationship with the Holy Spirit.

Brother will hand over brother to death, and the father his
30 child; children will rise up against parents and have them put to death. You will be hated by all because of my name. But the one who perseveres to the
35 end will be saved. (12 - 13)

We are told here that there will be a crucial urgency.

Perseverance can be obtained by taking to heart the teachings of Jesus.

When you see the desolating abomination standing where he should not (let the reader un-
40 derstand), then those in Judea must flee to the mountains, [and] a person on a housetop

This warning for the need to flee into safety is given by Jesus as He pinpoints a specific action by a certain individual. What this action is has been posited by some as the Anti-Christ taking

must not go down or enter to get anything out of his house, and a person in a field must not return to get his cloak. Woe to pregnant women and nursing mothers in those days. Pray that this does not happen in winter. For those times will have tribulation such as has not been since the beginning of God's creation until now, nor ever will be. If the Lord had not shortened those days, no one would be saved; but for the sake of the elect whom he chose, he did shorten the days. If anyone says to you then, 'Look, here is the Messiah! Look, there he is!' do not believe it. False messiahs and false prophets will arise and will perform signs and wonders in order to mislead, if that were possible, the elect. Be watchful! I have told it all to you beforehand. (14 - 23)

But in those days after that tribulation / the sun will be darkened, / and the moon will not give its light, / and the stars will be falling from the sky, / and the powers in the heavens will be shaken. / And then they will see 'the Son of Man coming in the clouds' with great power and glory, and then he will send out the angels and gather [his] elect from the four winds, from the end of the earth to the end of the sky.

Learn a lesson from the fig tree. When its branch becomes

over the Church by taking to himself its headship.

5

Jesus continues to exhort prayer as a means of obtaining help in these difficult times. 10

It is being commonly accepted that this generation is living in these times. These are some of the most serious words that Jesus 15 has given to His disciples of today.

The intensity of deception will 20 be so great that were not Jesus to come to our rescue, not one of His disciples could survive it.

25

These days will be so severe that all of nature will erupt as it prepares to present Jesus in His glorious return. 30

35

40

Understand that this is our God speaking to us. Never in the

tender and sprouts leaves, you know that summer is near. In the same way, when you see these things happening, know that he is near, at the gates. Amen, I say to you, this generation will not pass away until all these things have taken place. Heaven and earth will pass away, but my words will not pass away.

(24 – 31)

But of that day or hour, no one knows, neither the angels in heaven, nor the Son, but only the Father. Be watchful! Be alert! You do not know when the time will come. It is like a man traveling abroad. He leaves home and places his servants in charge, each with his work, and orders the gatekeeper to be on the watch. Watch, therefore; you do not know when the lord of the house is coming, whether in the evening, or at midnight, or at cockcrow, or in the morning. May he not come suddenly and find you sleeping. What I say to you, I say to all: 'Watch!'

(32 – 37)

Chapter 14

Watch and pray that you may not undergo the test. The spirit is willing but the flesh is weak.

(38)

Chapter 16

history of mankind have all these factors converged as they are doing in our day. The disciple of Jesus must take note and not be left behind. When we face the Lord there will be no excuses. After the cleansing of the evil in the world, the Lord Jesus will come in all of His glory and there will be an era of peace.

With these words Jesus is pleading with His disciples that they be on their guard. "Be watchful! Be alert!" This generation has been lulled to sleep by easy living, by lack of will power to withstand the evil one. Here there is no need to depend on private revelations. This is Jesus telling us as it will be. There will be no excuse on the part of His disciples, saying that they did not know. The word, as presented by Jesus is significant, "Watch."

Go into the whole world and proclaim the gospel to every creature. Whoever believes and is baptized will be saved; whoever does not believe will be condemned. These signs will accompany those who believe: in my name they will drive out demons, they will speak new languages. They will pick up serpents [with their hands], and if they drink any deadly thing, it will not harm them. They will lay hands on the sick, and they will recover. (15 – 18)

After the multiple warnings given to His followers, Jesus brings it all into the depth of hope. Nonetheless, it is all brought down to the internal experience of belief. Our generation is plagued by thought. Belief is found only in a few, the remnant. Taking Jesus' teachings to heart is what makes it possible for one to be His true disciple, and in so being, makes it possible for one ultimately to share the good news with others and enter into the kingdom.

Notes

Searching Through the Teachings of Jesus - - -

As Found in the Gospel of St. Luke

So as to Implant Them
into Your Heart

Chapter 4

Amen, I say to you, no prophet is accepted in his own native
5 place. Indeed, I tell you, there were many widows in Israel in the days of Elijah when the sky was closed for three and a half years and a severe famine spread
10 over the entire land. It was to none of these that Elijah was sent, but only to a widow in Zarephath in the land of Sidon. Again, there were many lepers
15 in Israel during the time of Elisha the prophet; yet not one of them was cleansed, but only Naaman the Syrian. (24 – 27)

20 To the other towns also I must proclaim the good news of the kingdom of God, because for this purpose I have been sent.
(43)
25

Today's disciples of Jesus will find that they too will be accepted more lovingly by those who are not of their own household. He reminds us that if He was persecuted, his followers must expect the same kind of treatment.

Chapter 5

What are you thinking in your hearts? Which is easier, to say,
30 'Your sins are forgiven,' or to say, 'Rise and walk?' But that you may know that the Son of Man has authority on earth to forgive sins -- ...I say to you, rise, pick
35 up your stretcher, and go home.
(22 – 24)

Jesus speaks in defense of who He is. It is acceptable for the disciple of Christ to put up a defense when his identity is in question.

Those who are healthy do not need a physician, but the sick
40 do. I have not come to call the righteous to repentance but sinners. (31-32)

Jesus defends Himself as to His purpose of coming into the world.

Can you make the wedding guests fast while the bridegroom is with them? But the days will come, and when the bridegroom is taken away from them, then they will fast in those days....No one tears a piece from a new cloak to patch an old one. Otherwise, he will tear the new and the piece from it will not match the old cloak. Likewise, no one pours new wine into old wineskins. Otherwise, the new wine will burst the skins, and it will be spilled, and the skins will be ruined. Rather, new wine must be poured into fresh wineskins. [And] no one who has been drinking old wine desires new, for he says, 'The old is good.'
(34 – 39)

Jesus defends His Apostles in that they were not fasting. There is, therefore, a time when the disciple of Jesus has a right to come forward in defending the behavior of others.

Chapter 6

"Have you not read what David did when he and those [who were] with him were hungry? [How] he went into the house of God, took the bread of offering, which only the priests could lawfully eat, ate of it, and shared it with his companions." Then he said to them, "The Son of Man is lord of the sabbath." (3 – 5)

I ask you, is it lawful to do good on the sabbath rather than to do evil, to save life rather than to destroy it? (9)

Here again, Jesus comes to the defense of His Apostles who were plucking grain on the Sabbath because they were hungry. The Pharisees, the leaders of the people, had multiplied laws and were hemming in the people so that they could scarcely move without failing to keep some specific law.

Blessed are you who are poor, / for the kingdom of God is yours.

The poor live in a state of dependency, which qualifies them for Jesus' kingdom.

5 Blessed are you who are now hungry, / for you will be satisfied.

This to speaks of a dependency which will be provided for.

Blessed are you who are now 10 weeping, / for you will laugh.

True weeping indicates sadness, which sadness will be taken away by living Jesus' way.

Blessed are you when people hate you, / and when they exclude and insult you, / and de-15 nounce your name as evil / on account of the Son of Man. / Rejoice and leap for joy on that day! / Behold, your reward / will be great in heaven. For 20 their / ancestors treated the prophets / in the same way. But woe to you who are rich, / for you have received your consolation. / But woe to you who are 25 filled now, / for you will be hungry. / Woe to you who laugh now, / for you will grieve and weep. / Woe to you when all speak well of you, / for their an-30 cestors treated the false / prophets in this way. (20 – 26)

It is reassuring to know that whatever suffering of persecution the followers of Jesus undergo because of one's affiliation with Jesus, they will be abundantly compensated.

Conversely, they who are well off, have no hunger, are filled with gladness, and are well spoken of, these have their fulfillment in this life and cannot therefore expect any reward in the life to come.

But to you who hear I say, love your enemies, do good to those 35 who hate you, bless those who curse you, pray for those who mistreat you. To the person who strikes you on one cheek, offer the other one as well, and from 40 the person who takes your cloak, do not withhold even your tunic. Give to everyone who

The followers of Jesus are to do good to those who hate them, bless those who curse them, pray for those who mistreat them. To those who do them harm, they are to turn to these and express acts of kindness instead.

asks of you, and from the one who takes what is yours do not demand it back. Do to others, as you would have them do to you. For if you love those who love you, what credit is that to you? Even sinners love those who love them. And if you do good to those who do good to you, what credit is that to you? Even sinners do the same. If you lend money to those from whom you expect repayment, what credit [is] that to you? Even sinners lend to sinners, and get back the same amount. But rather, love your enemies and do good to them, and lend expecting nothing back; then your reward will be great and you will be children of the Most High, for he himself is kind to the ungrateful and the wicked. Be merciful, just as [also] your Father is merciful. (27 – 36)

Stop judging and you will not be judged. Stop condemning and you will not be condemned. Forgive and you will be forgiven. Give and gifts will be given to you; a good measure, packed together, shaken down, and overflowing, will be poured into your lap. For the measure with which you measure will in return be measured out to you. (37 – 38)

Can a blind person guide a blind person? Will not both fall into a pit? No disciple is superior

Jesus' followers are exhorted to fill the needs of those who ask for help, and from those who take what is theirs, they are not to expect it back. They are to do to others what they would wish them to do to themselves. 5

Jesus' disciples are promised great rewards in His kingdom if they do good to those who do them harm. They are to imitate their heavenly Father, Who, Himself, does good to those who do not give to Him what He deserves. 10 15

As the Father is merciful, so too, Jesus expects His disciples to be merciful. 20

Jesus is saying to His disciples that they must expect the same treatment from the Father, as the treatment they direct towards their fellow men. 25

30

35

One cannot lead others unless one is qualified to do so. When the disciple is fully trained, he 40

to the teacher; but when fully trained, every disciple will be like his teacher. Why do you notice the splinter in your brother's eye, but do not perceive the wooden beam in your own? How can you say to your brother, 'Brother, let me remove that splinter in your eye,' when you do not even notice the wooden beam in your own eye? You hypocrite! Remove the wooden beam from your eye first; then you will see clearly to remove the splinter in your brother's eye. (39 – 42)

A good tree does not bear rotten fruit, nor does a rotten tree bear good fruit. For every tree is known by its own fruit. For people do not pick figs from thornbushes, nor do they gather grapes from brambles. A good person out of the store of goodness in his heart produces good, but an evil person out of a store of evil produces evil; for from the fullness of the heart the mouth speaks. (43 – 45)

Why do you call me, 'Lord, Lord,' but not do what I command? I will show you what someone is like who comes to me, listens to my words, and acts on them. That one is like a person building a house, who dug deeply and laid the foundation on rock; when the flood came, the river burst against that house but could not shake it because

becomes like the Master.

For the disciple to find fault with another person is not what should be done until and unless the disciple himself is without faults. Being so, he can more readily correct the faults of the other.

If there is goodness within a person, good actions will be forthcoming. A goodness or evil of a person can be measured by the good or evil acts that one performs.

From the fullness of the heart the mouth speaks. If the heart is filled with evil, one's speech will reflect evil; on the other hand, if the heart is filled with goodness, one will come forth with words of goodness.

If one listens to the words of the Lord and does not put them into practice, his soul will be lost. If on the other hand, after listening to the Lord's words, a person puts them into practice, his soul will be saved.

it had been well built. But the
one who listens and does not act
is like a person who built a house
on the ground without a foundation. When the river burst
against it, it collapsed at once
and was completely destroyed.
(46 – 49)

Chapter 7

Go and tell John what you
have seen and heard: the blind
regain their sight, the lame walk,
lepers are cleansed, the deaf hear,
the dead are raised, the poor
have the good news proclaimed
to them. And blessed is the one
who takes no offense at me.
(22 – 23)

What did you go out to the
desert to see -- a reed swayed by
the wind? Then what did you
go out to see? Someone dressed
in fine garments? Those who
dress luxuriously and live sumptuously are found in royal palaces. Then what did you go out
to see? A prophet? Yes, I tell you,
and more than a prophet. This
is the one about whom scripture
says: / 'Behold, I am sending my
messenger ahead of you, / he
will prepare your way before
you.' / I tell you, among those
born of women, no one is
greater than John; yet the least
in the kingdom of God is greater
than he. (24 – 28)

Then to what shall I compare

There has not been anyone born
of woman who is greater than
John the Baptist; however, the
one who is the least in the kingdom of God is greater than he.
This means that since Jesus'
coming into the world, he presented a way of life that is beyond that which John knew.

the people of this generation? What are they like? They are like children who sit in the market-place and call to one another, /
5 'We played the flute for you, but you did not dance. / We sang a dirge, but you did not weep.' / For John the Baptist came nei-ther eating food nor drinking
10 wine, and you said, 'He is pos-sessed by a demon.' The Son of Man came eating and drinking and you said, 'Look, he is a glut-ton and a drunkard, a friend of
15 tax collectors and sinners.' But wisdom is vindicated by all her children. (31 – 35)

Simon, I have something to
20 say to you....Two people were in debt to a certain creditor; one owed five hundred days' wages and the other owed fifty. Since they were unable to repay the
25 debt, he forgave it for both. Which of them will love him more?...You have judged rightly....Do you see this woman? When I entered your
30 house, you did not give me wa-ter for my feet, but she has bathed them with her tears and wiped them with her hair. You did not give me a kiss, but she
35 has not ceased kissing my feet since the time I entered. You did not anoint my head with oil, but she anointed my feet with oint-ment. So I tell you, her many
40 sins have been forgiven; hence, she has shown great love. But the one to whom little is for-

When a great sinner is converted to goodness, the love of God that is produced from this con-version is a great love. If one has few sins forgiven, his love of God is much less.

given, loves little. (40 – 47)

Chapter 8

A sower went out to sow his seed. And as he sowed, some seed fell on the path and was trampled, and the birds of the sky ate it up. Some seed fell on rocky ground, and when it grew, it withered for lack of moisture. Some seed fell among thorns, and the thorns grew with it and choked it. And some seed fell on good soil, and when it grew, it produced fruit a hundredfold. Whoever has ears to hear ought to hear. (5 – 8)

The words of Jesus are like seeds sown into the ground. Depending upon one's disposition to receive them, they will produce nothing by way of good works in one's life or they will produce either a limited amount of good works, a fair amount, or a plenitude.

Knowledge of the mysteries of the kingdom of God has been granted to you; but to the rest, they are made known through parables so that 'they may look but not see, and hear but not understand.' (10)

It is up to each individual to make an effort to learn what Jesus had to say, and do this with a great desire, or allow oneself to be content with knowing His teachings surface-wise only.

This is the meaning of the parable. The seed is the word of God. Those on the path are the ones who have heard, but the devil comes and takes away the word from their hearts that they may not believe and be saved. Those on rocky ground are the ones who, when they hear, receive the word with joy, but they have no root; they believe only for a time and fall away in time of trial. As for the seed that fell among thorns, they are the ones who have heard, but as they go

along, they are choked by the anxieties and riches and pleasures of life, and they fail to produce mature fruit. But as for the
5 seed that fell on rich soil, they are the ones who, when they have heard the word, embrace it with a generous and good heart, and bear fruit through
10 perseverance. (11 – 15)

No one who lights a lamp conceals it with a vessel or sets it under a bed; rather, he places
15 it on a lampstand so that those who enter may see the light. For there is nothing hidden that will not become visible, and nothing secret that will not be known
20 and come to light. Take care, then, how you hear. To anyone who has, more will be given, and from the one who has not, even what he seems to have will be
25 taken away. (16 – 18)

Light from the lamp is made to be seen and a source of light for a purpose. Our good deeds are to be a source of inspiration for others. Jesus also makes it known that everything that is hidden will ultimately be brought to light. Those who have, have through generosity and effort. These open the door for more. On God's part there is generosity, but if effort is not put forth, He cannot make use of it.

My mother and my brothers are those who hear the word of God and act on it. (21)
30

Jesus again places emphasis on the importance of carrying out His words into action.

Daughter, your faith has saved you; go in peace....Do not be afraid; just have faith and she will be saved. (48 – 50)
35

In these two statements, Jesus points out to everyone that it is faith that will bring on healing and a lasting state of peace.

Chapter 9

Take nothing for the journey, neither walking stick, nor sack,
40 nor food, nor money, and let no one take a second tunic. Whatever house you enter, stay there

Disciples are to go into the vineyard of evangelization trusting that all of their needs will be provided for.
The good news should never be

and leave from there. And as for those who do not welcome you, when you leave that town, shake the dust from your feet in testimony against them. (3 – 5)

The Son of Man must suffer greatly and be rejected by the elders, the chief priests, and the scribes, and be killed and on the third day be raised. (22)

If anyone wishes to come after me, he must deny himself and take up his cross daily and follow me. For whoever wishes to save his life will lose it, but whoever loses his life for my sake will save it. What profit is there for one to gain the whole world yet lose or forfeit himself? Whoever is ashamed of me and of my words, the Son of Man will be ashamed of when he comes in his glory and in the glory of the Father and of the holy angels. Truly I say to you, there are some standing here who will not taste death until they see the kingdom of God. (23 – 27)

Whoever receives this child in my name receives me, and whoever receives me receives the one who sent me. For the one who is least among all of you is the one who is the greatest. (48)

Do not prevent him, for whoever is not against you is for you. (50)

Foxes have dens and birds of

forced upon others. If they choose not to listen, the disciples are to move on.

Note here that Jesus informs His Apostles ahead of time of those things which will be done to Him.

The Master presents with a "must" the fact that His disciples are to take up their crosses. Whoever wishes to gain entrance into the Kingdom is to be absolutely detached from himself and place himself at His disposal.
Nothing in life is worth holding on to in preference to the saving of one's soul.

One is not to be ashamed of Jesus and His teachings. If this is done, Jesus will be ashamed of him before the Father and all of heaven.

Accepting children as being sent by God is tantamount to accepting Jesus and the Father. Littleness in spirit is what pleases God the most.

The total abandonment of self

the sky have nests, but the Son of Man has nowhere to rest his head....Follow me....Let the dead bury their dead. But you, go and proclaim the kingdom of God. (58 – 60)

No one who sets a hand to the plow and looks to what was left behind is fit for the kingdom of God. (62)

is what is expected by Jesus of His disciples. Their priority must be to put Him and His teachings at the head of all other activities.

Once the decision to put Jesus first in one's life is made, having second thoughts makes one unfit to dwell in His kingdom.

Chapter 10

The harvest is abundant but the laborers are few; so ask the master of the harvest to send out laborers for his harvest. Go on your way; behold, I am sending you like lambs among wolves. Carry no money bag, no sack, no sandals; and greet no one along the way. Into whatever house you enter, first say, 'Peace to this household.' If a peaceful person lives there, your peace will rest on him; but if not, it will return to you. Stay in the same house and eat and drink what is offered to you, for the laborer deserves his payment. Do not move about from one house to another. Whatever town you enter and they welcome you, eat what set before you, cure the sick in it and say to them, 'The kingdom of God is at hand for you.' Whatever town you enter and they do not receive you, go out into the streets and say, 'The dust of your town that clings to our feet, even

Praying for vocations is following through on the directive given by the Lord.

Jesus sends His Apostles out in meekness. They are to be trusting and carry nothing with them for their own sustenance. This is to be provided by those to whom they carry His words. They are not to move about but remain in the homes of peaceable listeners.

that we shake off against you.'
Yet know this: the kingdom of
God is at hand. I tell you, it will
be more tolerable for Sodom on
that day than for that town.
(2 – 12)

Woe to you, Chorazin! Woe
to you, Bethsaida! For if the
mighty deeds done in your
midst had been done in Tyre
and Sidon, they would long ago
have repented, sitting in sackcloth and ashes. But it will be
more tolerable for Tyre and
Sidon at the judgment than
for you. And as for you,
Capernaum, 'Will you be exalted to heaven? You will go
down to the netherworld.'
(13 – 15)

Whoever listens to you listens
to me. Whoever rejects you rejects me. And whoever rejects
me rejects the one who sent me.
(16)

When the disciple well trained
in the Word speaks, those who
listen, accept the Word, accept Jesus
and through Jesus, the Father.

I have observed Satan fall like
lightning from the sky. Behold,
I have given you the power 'to
tread upon serpents' and scor-
pions and upon the full force of
the enemy and nothing will
harm you. Nevertheless, do not
rejoice because the spirits are
subject to you, but rejoice because your names are written in
heaven. (18 – 20)

The disciples of Jesus do have
power over Satan. Their weapons are: humility, the Sacra-
ments, Sacramentals, the teaching of Jesus, of His Church,
Jesus' Mother, and the rite of
Exorcism. One may not rejoice
having this power, but may rejoice that God allows his disciples to have this power.

I give you praise, Father, Lord
of heaven and earth, for al-

Childlikeness comes about from
living the Gospel message. From

though you have hidden these things from the wise and the learned you have revealed them to the childlike. Yes, Father, such ⁵ has been your gracious will. All things have been handed over to me by my Father. No one knows who the Son is except the Father, and who the Father is ex-¹⁰ cept the Son and anyone to whom the Son wishes to reveal him....Blessed are the eyes that see what you see. For I say to you, many prophets and kings ¹⁵ desired to see what you see, but did not see it, and to hear what you hear, but did not hear it.

(21 – 24)

²⁰ A man fell victim to robbers as he went down from Jerusalem to Jericho. They stripped and beat him and went off leaving him half-dead. A priest hap-²⁵ pened to be going down that road, but when he saw him, he passed by on the opposite side. Likewise a Levite came to the place, and when he saw him, he ³⁰ passed by on the opposite side. But a Samaritan traveler who came upon him was moved with compassion at the sight. He approached the victim, poured oil ³⁵ and wine over his wounds and bandaged them. Then he lifted him up on his own animal, took him to an inn and cared for him. The next day he took out two ⁴⁰ silver coins and gave them to the innkeeper with the instruction, 'Take care of him. If you spend

it flows a simplicity wherein the individual is not divided against himself. There is no danger that the childlike person will fall in love with his own knowledge, will become blind to the truths presented by the Holy Spirit.

Through Jesus' teaching his followers are able to know truths which otherwise are hidden to everyone else.

Jesus teaches what true love of neighbor represents and demands.

more than what I have given you, I shall repay you on my way back.' Which of these three, in your opinion, was neighbor to the robbers' victim?...Go and do likewise. (30 – 37)

Martha, Martha, you are anxious and worried about many things....Mary has chosen the better part and it will not be taken from her. (41 – 42)

There is no condemnation of Martha here. Jesus simply sets forth priorities.

Chapter 11

When you pray, say: / Father, hallowed be your name, / your kingdom come. / Give us each day our daily bread / and forgive us our sins for we ourselves forgive everyone in debt to us, / and do not subject us to the final test. (2 – 4)

The basic elements of Christian living are found in prayer offered by Jesus.

Suppose one of you has a friend to whom he goes at midnight and says, 'Friend, lend me three loaves of bread, for a friend of mine has arrived at my house from a journey and I have nothing to offer him,' and he says in reply from within, 'Do not bother me; the door has already been locked and my children and I are already in bed. I cannot get up to give you anything.' I tell you, if he does not get up to give him the loaves because of their friendship, he will get up to give him whatever he needs because of his persistence. (5 – 8)

Herein Jesus teaches that when there is a real need, a disciple is encouraged to be humbly persistent with the Father.

5

10

15

20

25

30

35

40

And I tell you, ask and you will receive; seek and you will find; knock and the door will be opened to you. For everyone

5 who asks, receives; and the one who seeks, finds; and to the one who knocks, the door will be opened. (9 – 10)

10 What father among you would hand his son a snake when he asks for a fish? Or hand him a scorpion when he asks for an egg? If you then, who are

15 wicked, know how to give good gifts to your children, how much more will the Father in heaven give the holy Spirit to those who ask? (11 –13)

20

Every kingdom divided against itself will be laid waste and house will fall against house. And if Satan is divided against

25 himself, how will his kingdom stand? For you say that it is by Beelzebul that I drive out demons. If I, then, drive out demons by Beelzebul, by whom do

30 your own people drive them out? Therefore they will be your judges. But if it is by the finger of God that [I] drive out demons, then the kingdom of God

35 has come upon you. When a strong man fully armed guards his palace, his possessions are safe. But when one stronger than he attacks and overcomes

40 him, he takes away the armor on which he relied and distributes the spoils. Whoever is not with

This teaching merits Jesus' own words: "And I tell you, ask and you will receive; seek and you will find; knock and the door will be opened to you. For everyone who asks, receives; and the one who seeks, finds; and to the one who knocks, the door will be opened."

This is a tremendous revelation to anyone who wishes truly to follow Jesus in the most intimate way. "...How much more will the Father in heaven give the Holy Spirit to those who ask." If we ask for, and are granted the Holy Spirit, our life will become as that of Jesus. All that He did was prompted by Him.

Division is caused by Satan. This is one of his main weapons. Jesus points out that He is stronger than Satan. The two kingdoms are presently in the height and depth of the battle, a battle between goodness and evil, a battle between St. Michael and the fallen Lucifer. The followers of Jesus are caught in the crossfire.

Jesus puts forth the challenge: if one does not make one's commitment to Him, one will

me is against me, and whoever does not gather with me scatters. (17 – 23)

When an unclean spirit goes out of someone, it roams through arid regions searching for rest but, finding none, it says, 'I shall return to my home from which I came.' But upon returning, it finds it swept clean and put in order Then it goes and brings back seven other spirits more wicked than itself who move in and dwell there, and the last condition of that person is worse than the first. (24 – 26)

Rather, blessed are those who hear the word of God and observe it. (28)

This generation is an evil generation; it seeks a sign, but no sign will be given it, except the sign of Jonah. Just as Jonah became a sign to the Ninevites, so will the Son of Man be to this generation. At the judgment the queen of the south will rise with the men of this generation and she will condemn them, because she came from the ends of the earth to hear the wisdom of Solomon, and there is something greater than Solomon here. At the judgment the men of Nineveh will arise with this generation and condemn it, because at the preaching of Jonah they repented, and there is something greater than Jonah

conversely make it to Satan. It will be to one or the other. There will be no in between.

When through a conversion to Jesus one leaves the world of sin, there is the danger that the same one can fall deeper into sin because he has been cleansed and thus has a clearer mind and a will that is more free. Without prayer and penance, it is possible for the same one to fall deeper into sin because the temptations will be stronger and he would be more unaware.

Jesus affirms the great importance of following through on the Word having heard it.

Our own generation will have a difficult time to explain to the Father why we as a people did not more readily listen to His Son. We have been sent the Queen of the prophets, we have been given a Vicar of Christ who has been a channel of the greatest graces, we have experienced the Father's most generous mercy and still the hearts of most people are hard as stone. We are a stiff neck generation, a "no God" people.

here. (29 – 32)

No one who lights a lamp hides it away or places it [under a bushel basket], but on a lamp stand so that those who enter might see the light. The lamp of the body is your eye. When your eye is sound, then your whole body is filled with light, but when it is bad, then your body is in darkness. Take care, then, that the light in you not become darkness. If your whole body is full of light, and no part of it is in darkness, then it will be as full of light as a lamp illuminating you with its brightness. (33 –36)

If one would receive the light that comes from the Words of Jesus, his soul would be governed by the light of Christ which is the collection of His teachings. Once the soul lives by His teachings, it will be governed by the truth and the truth will set it free. In its freedom it would have the fullness of life which is joy. Once the soul would be flooded by joy, it lives a life of fullness.

Oh you Pharisees! Although you cleanse the outside of the cup and the dish, inside you are filled with plunder and evil. You fools! Did not the maker of the outside also make the inside? But as to what is within, give alms, and behold, everything will be clean for you. Woe to you Pharisees! You pay tithes of mint and of rue and of every garden herb, but you pay no attention to judgment and to love for God. These you should have done, without overlooking the others. Woe to you Pharisees! You love the seat of honor in synagogues and greetings in marketplaces. Woe to you! You are like unseen graves over which people unknowingly walk. (39 – 44)

In directing His "Woes" toward the Pharisees, Jesus gives His disciples lessons on how not to be hypocritical, how to behave in life in such a way as to give Him honor and glory.

Woe also to you scholars of the law! You impose on people burdens hard to carry, but you yourselves do not lift one finger to touch them. Woe to you! You build the memorials of the prophets whom your ancestors killed. Consequently, you bear witness and give consent to the deeds of your ancestors, for they killed them and you do the building. Therefore, the wisdom of God said, 'I will send to them prophets and apostles; some of them they will kill and perse-cute' in order that this genera-tion might be charged with the blood of all the prophets shed since the foundation of the world, from the blood of Abel to the blood of Zechariah who died between the altar and the temple building. Yes, I tell you, this generation will be charged with their blood! Woe to you, scholars of the law! You have taken away the key of knowl-edge. You yourselves did not enter and you stopped those try-ing to enter. (46 – 52)

It was this very approach that Jesus took toward the leaders and the learned that ultimately caused His death. On the other hand, He could not merely ig-nore their behavior. He had to put the axe to the roots of the tree. The true disciple has the duty to be faithful to Christ, and therefore is to go forward to fight the battle against evil.

Chapter 12

Beware of the leaven -- that is, the hypocrisy -- of the Phari-sees. (1)

The true disciple of Jesus must have no hidden agenda.

There is nothing concealed that will not be revealed, nor secret that will not be known. There-fore whatever you have said in the darkness will be heard in the

This teaching of Jesus is frighten-ing! Does it mean that all of our secret thoughts and sins will be made known? It would seem that all of our confessed sins will not.

light, and what you have whispered behind closed doors will be proclaimed on the housetops. I tell you, my friends, do not be afraid of those who kill the body but after that can do no more. I shall show you whom to fear. Be afraid of the one who after killing has the power to cast into Gehenna; yes, I tell you, be afraid of that one. Are not five sparrows sold for two small coins? Yet not one of them has escaped the notice of God. Even the hairs of your head have all been counted. Do not be afraid. You are worth more than many sparrows. (2 – 7)

This has reference to martyrdom. No need to fear this. The Holy Spirit will be at our side every second to give us strength to see it through.

Only God has the power to throw anyone into Gehenna. For those who fear God there is no need to fear. His love is infinite and everlasting.

I tell you, everyone who acknowledges me before others the Son of Man will acknowledge before the angels of God. But whoever denies me before others will be denied before the angels of God.
Everyone who speaks a word against the Son of Man will be forgiven, but the one who blasphemes against the holy Spirit will not be forgiven. (8 – 10)

Each person is given the opportunity to make a decision for Jesus or against Jesus. For the first there will be the eternal reward, for the second, eternal punishment.

One who speaks against the Holy Spirit cannot be forgiven because He is the source of forgiveness. One cuts the hand that feeds him.

When they take you before synagogues and before rulers and authorities, do not worry about how or what your defense will be or about what you are to say. For the holy Spirit will teach you at that moment what you should say. (11 – 12)

The Holy Spirit is the source of truth and courage. When in difficulty because of one's discipleship, the Spirit will be on hand to give both.

Friend, who appointed me as

your judge and arbitrator? …Take care to guard against all greed, for though one may be rich, one's life does not consist of possessions. (14 – 15)

There was a rich man whose land produced a bountiful harvest. He asked himself, 'What shall I do, for I do not have space to store my harvest?' And he said, 'This is what I shall do: I shall tear down my barns and build larger ones. There I shall store all my grain and other goods and I shall say to myself, 'Now as for you, you have so many good things stored up for many years, rest, eat, drink, be merry!' But God said to him, 'You fool, this night your life will be demanded of you; and the things you have prepared, to whom will they belong?' Thus will it be for the one who stores up treasure for himself but is not rich in what matters to God. (16 – 21)

Therefore I tell you, do not worry about your life and what you will eat, or about your body and what you will wear. For life is more than food and the body more than clothing. Notice the ravens: they do not sow or reap; they have neither storehouse nor barn, yet God feeds them. How much more important are you than birds! Can any of you by worrying add a moment to your life-span? If even the smallest

Life is greater than riches. Greed overpowers one's sense of justice and truth.

Riches will not enter into one's discussion with God at the end of one's life. How they were used will. The disciple is being taught that it is foolish to place all of one's trust on the worldly things that one has amassed. Possessions mean nothing to God. One's attitude towards them and how one has used them will.

Followers of Jesus are to have trust in the loving Father who provides all the needs of His creatures. This does not mean that the follower can go into total carefreeness. All creatures are to work together with God in this providing. The robin works at pulling the worm out of the earth. The father bear goes out looking for food to feed mother bear and the little bears. The message is that human beings

things are beyond your control, why are you anxious about the rest? Notice how the flowers grow. They do not toil or spin. 5 But I tell you, not even Solomon in all his splendor was dressed like one of them. If God so clothes the grass in the field that grows today and is thrown into 10 the oven tomorrow, will he not much more provide for you, O you of little faith? As for you, do not seek what you are to eat and what you are to drink, and 15 do not worry anymore. All the nations of the world seek for these things, and your Father knows that you need them. Instead, seek his kingdom, and 20 these other things will be given you besides. Do not be afraid any longer, little flock, for your Father is pleased to give you the kingdom. Sell your belongings 25 and give alms. Provide money bags for yourselves that do not wear out, an inexhaustible treasure in heaven that no thief can reach nor moth destroy. For 30 where your treasure is, there also will your heart be. (22 – 34)

Gird your loins and light your lamps and be like servants who 35 await their master's return from a wedding, ready to open immediately when he comes and knocks. Blessed are those servants whom the master finds 40 vigilant on his arrival. Amen, I say to you, he will gird himself, have them recline at table, and

must still cooperate with God in this providing. When one is out of work and needs work to provide for the family, one is to pray for enlightenment as to where to seek work and for the energy to pursue all possibilities.

.

The disciple is being taught by the Master that he is to seek the kingdom of God first and all of his needs will be provided for, not that they will all come down from heaven in a parachute, but all means to provide the essentials of life will be provided by the loving and caring Father.

The simple lesson that is given by Jesus is that even in today's day the disciple must be alert, wide awake and prepared for the coming of Jesus in His glorious return. There is no doubt about it, the disciple of today is closer to that event than anyone in history has ever been. The alertness must be more intensified as

proceed to wait on them. And should he come in the second or third watch and find them prepared in this way, blessed are those servants. Be sure of this: if the master of the house had known the hour when the thief was coming, he would not have let his house be broken into. You also must be prepared, for at an hour you do not expect, the Son of Man will come. (35 – 40)

Who, then, is the faithful and prudent steward whom the master will put in charge of his servants to distribute [the] food allowance at the proper time? Blessed is that servant whom his master on arrival finds doing so. Truly, I say to you, he will put him in charge of all his property. But if that servant says to himself, 'My master is delayed in coming,' and begins to beat the menservants and the maidservants, to eat and drink and get drunk, then that servant's master will come on an unexpected day and at an unknown hour and will punish him severely and assign him a place with the unfaithful. That servant who knew his master's will but did not make preparations nor act in accord with his will shall be beaten severely; and the servant who was ignorant of his master's will but acted in a way deserving of a severe beating shall be beaten only lightly. Much will be required of the

one passes through life year by year, and day by day.

5

Another parable points to the same warning. One is to keep awake, continue fulfilling one's responsibilities faithfully, live by faith, trust and love and keep on 10 day by day awaiting the great day of Jesus' return.

15

20

Those who have been informed 25 of the Lord's glorious return and have made no preparation for it, will be made to pay for their lack of concern.

30

For those who have received much, much will be demanded. 35

Jesus had come to bring love into the world. Loving is what 40 His disciples must make an effort to do. Jesus had also come

person entrusted with much, and still more will be demanded of the person entrusted with more. (42 – 48)

to atone for man's sins. He knew what this meant, that He would have to undergo death.

5

I have come to set the earth on fire, and how I wish it were already blazing! There is a baptism with which I must be baptized, and how great is my anguish until it is accomplished! Do you think that I have come to establish peace on the earth? No, I tell you, but rather division. From now on a household of five will be divided, three against two and two against three; a father will be divided against his son and a son against his father, a mother against her daughter and a daughter against her mother, a mother-in-law against her daughter-in-law and a daughter-in-law against her mother-in-law. (49 – 53)

Human beings have free will. Jesus had come upon the earth to bring oneness to mankind, bonded by love. Nonetheless, because of man's free will, He knew that some within the same family would choose Him and others would not.

When you see [a] cloud rising in the west you say immediately that it is going to rain -- and so it does; and when you notice that the wind is blowing from the south you say that it is going to be hot -- and so it is. You hypocrites! You know how to interpret the appearance of the earth and the sky; why do you not know how to interpret the present time? (54 – 56)

The Messiah had come into the midst of the chosen people and yet the leaders did not recognize Him.

Why do you not judge for yourselves what is right? If you are to go with your opponent

Jesus encourages His followers to settle difficulties out of court, to do so peacefully.

before a magistrate, make an effort to settle the matter on the way; otherwise your opponent will turn you over to the judge, and the judge hand you over to the constable, and the constable throw you into prison. I say to you, you will not be released until you have paid the last penny. (57 – 59)

Chapter 13

Do you think that because these Galileans suffered in this way they were greater sinners than all other Galileans? By no means! But I tell you, if you do not repent, you will all perish as they did! Or those eighteen people who were killed when the tower at Siloam fell on them -- do you think they were more guilty than everyone else who lived in Jerusalem? By no means! But I tell you, if you do not repent, you will all perish as they did! (2 – 5)

There once was a person who had a fig tree planted in his orchard, and when he came in search of fruit on it but found none, he said to the gardener, 'For three years now I have come in search of fruit on this fig tree but have found none. [So] cut it down. Why should it exhaust the soil?' He said to him in reply, 'Sir, leave it for this year also, and I shall cultivate the ground around it and fertilize it;

Simply because there are those who have fallen into some grave hardship, it does not mean that what happened was because they were in sin. On the other hand, those who are in sin and do not repent can expect the Lord to come forth with justice.

The disciples of Jesus are expected to produce good fruit. They do have sources at their finger tips to make use of in order that this would be done. If they do not make use of these sources, it is not possible for them to accomplish that which the Master prepared them for. In their failure to produce good fruits, the Master will offer special help. If, after that, they do not do any better, they will be

it may bear fruit in the future. If not you can cut it down.'
(6 – 9)

⁵   Hypocrites! Does not each one of you on the sabbath untie his ox or his ass from the manger and lead it out for watering? This daughter of Abraham, ¹⁰ whom Satan has bound for eighteen years now, ought she not to have been set free on the sabbath day from this bondage?
(15 – 16)

¹⁵

What is the kingdom of God like? To what can I compare it? It is like a mustard seed that a person took and planted in the ²⁰ garden. When it was fully grown, it became a large bush and 'the birds of the sky dwelt in its branches.' (18 – 19)

²⁵   To what shall I compare the kingdom of God? It is like yeast that a woman took and mixed [in] with three measures of wheat flour until the whole ³⁰ batch of dough was leavened.
(20 – 21)

Strive to enter through the narrow gate, for many, I tell you, ³⁵ will attempt to enter but will not be strong enough. After the master of the house has arisen and locked the door, then will you stand outside knocking and ⁴⁰ saying, 'Lord, open the door for us.' He will say to you in reply, 'I do not know where you are

cut out of an entry into the Kingdom.

Being hypocritical is something that the Lord loathes in His followers. The leaders made laws for the people which they themselves did not observe.

Belonging to the kingdom of God means that there will be much good accomplished.

There must be effort put forth in order that one follows the teachings of Jesus.

Jesus once again points out to the leaders that they will be missing out in entering the kingdom because they fail to do those things which they should be doing to be of assistance to

from.' And you will say, 'We ate and drank in your company and you taught in our streets.' Then he will say to you, 'I do not know where [you] are from. Depart from me, all you evildoers!' And there will be wailing and grinding of teeth when you see Abraham, Isaac, and Jacob and all the prophets in the kingdom of God and you yourselves cast out. And people will come from the east and the west and from the north and the south and will recline at table in the kingdom of God. For behold, some are last who will be first, and some are first who will be last. (24 – 30)

Go and tell that fox, 'Behold, I cast out demons and I perform healings today and tomorrow, and on the third day I accomplish my purpose. Yet I must continue on my way today, tomorrow, and the following day, for it is impossible that a prophet should die outside of Jerusalem.' (32 – 33)

Jerusalem, Jerusalem, you who kill the prophets and stone those sent to you, how many times I yearned to gather your children together as a hen gathers her brood under her wings, but you were unwilling! Behold, your house will be abandoned. [But] I tell you, you will not see me until [the time comes when] you say, 'Blessed is he who

the people. The time will come when because they failed to recognize Him, others will be invited and they will be left outside. 5

As leaders of the people, the Pharisees will lose their prominence while others without authority or importance will take a lead and enter the kingdom. 15

20

25

30

Jesus laments over Jerusalem because it by and large had not recognized Him for Who He really was. 35

He foretells that Jerusalem will 40 be destroyed and the city will be abandoned.

comes in the name of the Lord.'
(34 – 35)

Chapter 14

5

Who among you, if your son or ox falls into a cistern, would not immediately pull him out on the sabbath day? (5)

10

When you are invited by someone to a wedding banquet, do not recline at table in the place of honor. A more distin-
15 guished guest than you may have been invited by him, and the host who invited both of you may approach you and say, 'Give your place to this man,'
20 and then you would proceed with embarrassment to take the lowest place. Rather, when you are invited, go and take the lowest place so that when the host
25 comes to you he may say, 'My friend, move up to a higher position.' Then you will enjoy the esteem of your companions at the table. For everyone who ex-
30 alts himself will be humbled, but the one who humbles himself will be exalted. (8 – 11)

When you hold a lunch or a
35 dinner, do not invite your friends or your brothers or your relatives or your wealthy neighbors, in case they may invite you back and you have repayment.
40 Rather, when you hold a banquet, invite the poor, the crippled, the lame, the blind;

Honors are something that the disciples of Jesus should not aspire to.

When performing acts of kindness, one should not look to be reciprocated. It is better to express kindness to those who are truly in need. From these one should not look to receive any

blessed indeed will you be because of their inability to repay you. For you will be repaid at the resurrection of the righteous. (12 – 14)

A man gave a great dinner to which he invited many. When the time for the dinner came, he dispatched his servant to say to those invited, 'Come, everything is now ready.' But one by one, they all began to excuse themselves. The first said to him, 'I have purchased a field and must go to examine it; I ask you, consider me excused.' And another said, 'I have purchased five yoke of oxen and am on my way to evaluate them; I ask you, consider me excused.' And another said, 'I have just married a woman, and therefore I cannot come.' The servant went and reported this to his master. Then the master of the house in a rage commanded his servant, 'Go out quickly into the streets and alleys of the town and bring in here the poor and the crippled, the blind and the lame.' The servant reported, 'Sir, your orders have been carried out and still there is room.' The master then ordered the servant, 'Go out to the highways and hedgerows and make people come in that my home may be filled. For, I tell you, none of those men who were invited will taste my dinner.' (16 – 24)

type of compensation.

5

Jesus directs this parable against the leaders of His people who had not accepted the invitation to enter the kingdom. As a result, the Lord God extended this same invitation to others, others who were not members of the select group.

10

15

The learned had all types of excuses against bending to Jesus in respect for Who He was. Jesus directed Himself, His teachings and His miracles to the ordinary people, and even to those whom the educated leaders considered as sinners and breakers of the law.

20

25

30

This parable also serves as a prophecy directed to the future when an invitation to the kingdom was extended to the Gentiles.

35

40

If any one comes to me without hating his father and mother, wife and children, brothers and sisters, and even his
5 own life, he cannot be my disciple. Whoever does not carry his own cross and come after me cannot be my disciple. Which of you wishing to construct a
10 tower does not first sit down and calculate the cost to see if there is enough for its completion? Otherwise, after laying the foundation and finding himself
15 unable to finish the work the onlookers should laugh at him and say, 'This one began to build but did not have the resources to finish.' Or what king
20 marching into battle would not first sit down and decide whether with ten thousand troops he can successfully oppose another king advancing
25 upon him with twenty thousand troops? But if not, while he is still far away, he will send a delegation to ask for peace terms. In the same way, everyone of
30 you who does not renounce all his possessions cannot be my disciple. (26 – 33)

Jesus' invitation to discipleship is strict indeed. He demands first of all that one put Him first in one's life, making Him and His teaching more important than even mother and father.

Secondly, he makes clear that anyone who wishes to be His disciple must accept a responsibility of suffering. The cross is to be an integral part of the true disciple.

Salt is good, but if salt itself
35 loses its taste, with what can its flavor be restored? It is fit neither for the soil nor for the manure pile; it is thrown out. Whoever has ears to hear ought to
40 hear. (34 – 35)

A follower without a solid conviction of Who Jesus is and what constitutes His mission and His teachings does not have the calling as a true disciple.

Chapter 15

What man among you having a hundred sheep and losing one of them would not leave the ninety-nine in the desert and go after the lost one until he finds it? And when he does find it, he sets it on his shoulders with great joy and, upon his arrival home, he calls together his friends and neighbors and says to them, 'Rejoice with me because I have found my lost sheep.' I tell you, in just the same way there will be more joy in heaven over one sinner who repents than over ninety-nine righteous people who have no need of repentance.

Or what woman having ten coins and losing one would not light a lamp and sweep the house, searching carefully until she finds it? And when she does find it, she calls together her friends and neighbors and says to them, 'Rejoice with me because I have found the coin that I lost.' In just the same way, I tell you, there will be rejoicing among the angels of God over one sinner who repents. (4 – 7)

A man had two sons, and the younger son said to his father, 'Father, give me the share of your estate that should come to me.' So the father divided the property between them. After a few days, the younger son collected all his belongings and set off to a distant country where he squandered his inheritance on a life of dissipation.

The mercy of Jesus is infinite. He constantly searches for the sinner as the "Hound of Heaven," to offer encouragement. The disciple can find hope in this should he ever have fears of straying away from the fold.

It is good to learn here that those in heaven are aware of what goes on earth and rejoice even over the conversion of one sinner.

Here again one is reminded to what extent the Father will go to welcome back into the fold each person who repents of his sins.

When he had freely spent everything, a severe famine struck that country, and he found himself in dire need. So he hired himself out to one of the local citizens who sent him to his farm to tend the swine. And he longed to eat his fill of the pods on which the swine fed, but nobody gave him any. Coming to his senses he thought, 'How many of my father's hired workers have more than enough food to eat, but here am I, dying from hunger. I shall get up and go to my father and I shall say to him, 'Father, I have sinned against heaven and against you. I no longer deserve to be called your son; treat me as you would treat one of your hired workers.' So he got up and went back to his father. While he was still a long way off, his father caught sight of him, and was filled with compassion. He ran to his son, embraced him and kissed him. His son said to him, 'Father, I have sinned against heaven and against you; I no longer deserve to be called your son.' But his father ordered his servants, 'Quickly bring the finest robe and put it on him; put a ring on his finger and sandals on his feet. Take the fattened calf and slaughter it. Then let us celebrate with a feast, because this son of mine was dead, and has come to life again; he was lost, and has been found.' Then the celebration began. Now the older son had been out in the field and, on his way back, as he neared the house, he heard the sound of music and dancing. He called one of the servants and asked what this might mean. The servant said to him, 'Your brother has returned and your father has slaughtered the fattened calf because he has him back safe and sound.' He became angry, and when he refused to enter the house, his father came out and pleaded with him. He said to his father in reply, 'Look, all these years I served you and not once did I disobey your orders; yet you never gave me even a young goat to feast on with my friends. But when your son returns who swallowed up your property with prostitutes, for him you slaughter the fattened calf.' He said to him, 'My son, you are here with me always; everything I have is yours. But now we must celebrate and rejoice, because your brother was dead and has come to life again; he was lost and has been found.' (11 – 32)

Chapter 16

A rich man had a steward who was reported to him for squandering his property. He summoned him and said, 'What is this I hear about you? Prepare a full account of your stewardship, because you can no longer be my steward.' The steward said

Jesus presents a scenario of a person who has fallen out of favor with his employer. The lesson is, how on the natural level one would go to preserve himself in the good standing of others for one's own survival. This is done through human prudence.

to himself, 'What shall I do, now that my master is taking the position of steward away from me? I am not strong enough to
5 dig and I am ashamed to beg. I know what I shall do so that, when I am removed from the stewardship, they may welcome me into their homes.' He called
10 in his master's debtors one by one. To the first he said, 'How much do you owe my master?' He replied, 'One hundred measures of olive oil.' He said to
15 him, 'Here is your promissory note. Sit down and quickly write one for fifty.' Then to another he said, 'And you, how much do you owe?' He replied, 'One
20 hundred kors of wheat.' He said to him, 'Here is your promissory note; write one for eighty.' And the master commended that dishonest steward for act-
25 ing prudently.

For the children of this world are more prudent in dealing with their own generation than are the children of light. I tell
30 you, make friends for yourselves with dishonest wealth, so that when it fails, you will be welcomed into eternal dwellings. The person who is trustworthy
35 in very small matters is also trustworthy in great ones; and the person who is dishonest in very small matters is also dishonest in great ones. If, therefore,
40 you are not trustworthy with dishonest wealth, who will trust you with true wealth? If you are

This discourse on the leeway that the dishonest person has is brought to a main point that one cannot trust a person at all even if he is dishonest only in little things. On the other hand, Jesus points out that a person who is honest in little things can be trusted in big things too.

not trustworthy with what belongs to another, who will give you what is yours? (1 – 12)

No servant can serve two masters. He will either hate one and love the other, or be devoted to one and despise the other. You cannot serve God and mammon. (13)

The Master brings life to the need of a decision on the part of each person. Is God to be first in one's life or should it be money?

You justify yourselves in the sight of others, but God knows your hearts; for what is of human esteem is an abomination in the sight of God.

The law and the prophets lasted until John; but from then on the kingdom of God is proclaimed, and everyone who enters does so with violence. It is easier for heaven and earth to pass away than for the smallest part of a letter of the law to become invalid. (15 – 17)

We are only what we are in the sight of the Lord.

One has to put forth effort, swim against the current of one's natural instincts, in order to enter into the kingdom of God.

God's law does not, and will not change.

Everyone who divorces his wife and marries another commits adultery, and the one who marries a woman divorced from her husband commits adultery. (18)

God's law about marriage is solid. If a marriage is valid, it is to last until death do they part. Modern man has drifted far from this law and, therefore, far from God.

There was a rich man who dressed in purple garments and fine linen and dined sumptuously each day. And lying at his door was a poor man named Lazarus, covered with sores, who would gladly have eaten his fill of the scraps that fell from the rich man's table. Dogs even used

An issue is brought up that has caused a number of disciples to be concerned about. It is: how is it that people who do not worship God seem to have it so good in life, and conversely, how

to come and lick his sores. When the poor man died, he was carried away by angels to the bosom of Abraham. The rich
5 man also died and was buried, and from the netherworld, where he was in torment, he raised his eyes and saw Abraham far off and Lazarus at his side.
10 And he cried out, 'Father Abraham, have pity on me. Send Lazarus to dip the tip of his finger in water and cool my tongue, for I am suffering tor-
15 ment in these flames.' Abraham replied, 'My child, remember that you received what was good during your lifetime while Lazarus likewise received what
20 was bad; but now he is comforted here, whereas you are tormented. Moreover, between us and you a great chasm is established to prevent anyone from
25 crossing who might wish to go from our side to yours or from your side to ours.' He said, 'Then I beg you, father, send him to my father's house, for I
30 have five brothers, so that he may warn them, lest they too come to this place of torment.' But Abraham replied, 'They have Moses and the prophets.
35 Let them listen to them.' He said, 'Oh no, father Abraham, but if someone from the dead goes to them, they will repent.' Then Abraham said, 'If they will
40 not listen to Moses and the prophets, neither will they be persuaded if someone should

is it that people who worship God often have a very difficult life?

Jesus gives an insight to His disciples as to how things are in the nether world, that is, there is no passage from where the condemned are to those in heaven.

Secondly, He keenly put forth the truth that if people who have turned their back on God do not themselves make a decision to turn to Him, not even if some one would come from the dead to remind them of their obligation to God, would they be moved by fear to put themselves into God's good favor.

rise from the dead.' (19 – 31)

Chapter 17

Things that cause sin will inevitably occur, but woe to the person through whom they occur. It would be better for him if a millstone were put around his neck and he be thrown into the sea than for him to cause one of these little ones to sin. Be on your guard! If your brother sins, rebuke him; and if he repents, forgive him. And if he wrongs you seven times in one day and returns to you seven times saying, 'I am sorry,' you should forgive him. (1 – 4)

Responsibility not to sin resides 5 within each individual. Mankind has been endowed with a will that is free. This means that each person has the power of decision either to sin or not. 10 Little ones are the innocent ones. To cause one of these to sin is a serious matter.

Jesus mentions forgiveness a 15 number of times in the Scripture. It is a most important inner action that the disciple must make use of.

20

If you have faith the size of a mustard seed, you would say to [this] mulberry tree, 'Be uprooted and planted in the sea,' and it would obey you. (6)

Even a little faith can accomplish great things. It is an inner experience of the heart which connects one immediately with God, the angels and all the saints. 25

Who among you would say to your servant who has just come in from plowing or tending sheep in the field, 'Come here immediately and take your place at table?' Would he not rather say to him, 'Prepare something for me to eat. Put on your apron and wait on me while I eat and drink. You may eat and drink when I am finished'? Is he grateful to that servant because he did what was commanded? So should it be with you. When you have done all you have been commanded, say, 'We are un-

30

A desire for approval, seeking some compensation for a good work done, is one of the easiest 35 human actions to slip into. Jesus sets His disciples straight. It is always a duty to be loving and to express love in being helpful to those in need. 40

profitable servants; we have done what we were obliged to do.' (7 – 10)

5   The coming of the kingdom of God cannot be observed, and no one will announce, 'Look, here it is,' or, 'There it is.' For behold, the kingdom of God is 10 among you....The days will come when you will long to see one of the days of the Son of Man, but you will not see it. There will be those who will say 15 to you, 'Look, there he is,' [or] 'Look, here he is.' Do not go off, do not run in pursuit. For just as lightning flashes and lights up the sky from one side to the 20 other, so will the Son of Man be [in his day]. But first he must suffer greatly and be rejected by this generation. As it was in the days of Noah, so it will be in the 25 days of the Son of Man; they were eating and drinking, marrying and giving in marriage up to the day that Noah entered the ark, and the flood came and de- 30 stroyed them all. Similarly, as it was in the days of Lot: they were eating, drinking, buying, selling, planting, building; on the day when Lot left Sodom, fire and 35 brimstone rained from the sky to destroy them all. So it will be on the day the Son of Man is revealed. On that day, a person who is on the housetop and 40 whose belongings are in the house must not go down to get them, and likewise a person in

The kingdom of God is within a person; the kingdom of God is among you. It cannot be observed by looking about for it.

Jesus is to come into the world a second time. This is certain. Only the Father knows when this will be. Nonetheless, Jesus did chide the Apostles and the Pharisees for not recognizing the signs of the times.

There will be a preparation needed before the glorious coming of Jesus will take place as there was a preparation that Noah had to undertake. What happened in his time will happen again; people will be so occupied that they will lose out as did the people when the flood finally came.

Jesus' Second Coming will be accompanied by a crisis and an air of emergency. Fast decisions will have to be made.

the field must not return to what was left behind. Remember the wife of Lot. Whoever seeks to preserve his life will lose it, but whoever loses it will save it. I tell you, on that night there will be two people in one bed; one will be taken, the other left. And there will be two women grinding meal together; one will be taken, the other left.…Where the body is, there also the vultures will gather. (20 – 37)

If the Second Coming is to be a glorious return, it means that He comes back as a Victor. All of His enemies will have had to be conquered beforehand. This means that there will be an external powerful force. Vultures are creatures who look for and live on the spoils.

Chapter 18

"There was a judge in a certain town who neither feared God nor respected any human being. And a widow in that town used to come to him and say, 'Render a just decision for me against my adversary.' For a long time the judge was unwilling, but eventually he thought, 'While it is true that I neither fear God nor respect any human being, because this widow keeps bothering me I shall deliver a just decision for her lest she finally come and strike me.'" The Lord said, "Pay attention to what the dishonest judge says. Will not God then secure the rights of his chosen ones who call out to him day and night? Will he be slow to answer them? I tell you, he will see to it that justice is done for them speedily. But when the Son of Man comes, will he find faith on earth?" (2 – 8)

Jesus makes use of this explicitly clear parable to put an important point across to His flock. It was because of the persistence of the widow that she was finally given her due. The Father is always on the lookout for those of our day who are being treated unjustly. He is the God of justice as He is also the God of mercy. He responds quickly to a request made by one who is being unjustly treated.

Jesus equates the urgent plea with the heart quality of faith. In our high powered age of super intellection, one can readily understand the pertinence of His question.

Two people went up to the temple area to pray; one was a Pharisee and the other was a tax collector. The Pharisee took up
5 his position and spoke this prayer to himself, 'O God, I thank you that I am not like the rest of humanity -- greedy, dishonest, adulterous -- or even like
10 this tax collector. I fast twice a week, and I pay tithes on my whole income.' But the tax collector stood off at a distance and would not even raise his eyes to
15 heaven but beat his breast and prayed, 'O God, be merciful to me a sinner.' I tell you, the latter went home justified, not the former; for everyone who exalts
20 himself will be humbled, and the one who humbles himself will be exalted. (10 – 14)

This picturesque episode gives a clear indication of what one's inner attitude should be when praying. It is to be a stance of humility, a stance of honest truth, as compared with a haughty and inconsiderate presentation.

Jesus gives a clear indication that the Father will takes His own initiative to humble the proud and exult the humble.

Let the children come to me
25 and do not prevent them; for the kingdom of God belongs to such as these. Amen, I say to you, whoever does not accept the kingdom of God like a child
30 will not enter it. (16 – 17)

Jesus welcomes children with extended arms and an open heart. He is not placing importance on the smallness of the body but rather on the humility of the soul. It is this quality of the child that one must have to enter the kingdom.

Why do you call me good? No one is good but God alone. (19)

35 You know the commandments, 'You shall not commit adultery; you shall not kill; you shall not steal; you shall not bear false witness; honor your father
40 and your mother.'…There is still one thing left for you: sell all that you have and distribute it

There are grades of goodness. To live a life according to what is expected by obeying the Ten Commandments is basic goodness. There are additional levels. To detach oneself from all of one's attachments in order to be completely attached to Jesus

to the poor, and you will have a treasure in heaven. Then come, follow me….How hard it is for those who have wealth to enter the kingdom of God! For it is easier for a camel to pass through the eye of a needle than for a rich person to enter the kingdom of God….What is impossible for human beings is possible for God. (20 – 27)

Amen, I say to you, there is no one who has given up house or wife or brothers or parents or children for the sake of the kingdom of God who will not receive [back] an over abundant return in this present age and eternal life in the age to come. (29 – 30)

Behold, we are going up to Jerusalem and everything written by the prophets about the Son of Man will be fulfilled. He will be handed over to the Gentiles and he will be mocked and insulted and spat upon; and after they have scourged him they will kill him, but on the third day he will rise. (31 – 33)

Chapter 19

A nobleman went off to a distant country to obtain the kingship for himself and then to return. He called ten of his servants and gave them ten gold coins and told them, 'Engage in trade with these until I return.'

alone introduces one to a higher level of holiness. For a soul to aspire to love God with one's whole heart, mind, and strength is on the way to the peak of holiness. The allurement of riches is an obstacle to total detachment. With grace, one can use riches as a means to an end instead of as an end in itself.

Jesus makes it clear that a disciple who leaves all and puts Him first, will be compensated not only in this life, but also in the life to come. After a total gift of self to Him, one can return to his attachments, but now make use of them selflessly, for God's greater honor and glory.

To realize that Jesus knew ahead of time all that He would have to undergo, and still lived His day to day life filled with love and surrender to His Father's Will, can be a source of inspiration to His followers. Yes, He was God, but in His human nature, his life was as is ours, except it was free from all sin.

The parable before us is a clear lesson to His listeners as to of what it means to be spiritually industrious. Depending upon what gifts a person receives from God, he is to respond accordingly in the use of them. To one

His fellow citizens, however, despised him and sent a delegation after him to announce, 'We do not want this man to be our
5 king.' But when he returned after obtaining the kingship, he had the servants called, to whom he had given the money, to learn what they had gained by trad-
10 ing. The first came forward and said, 'Sir, your gold coin has earned ten additional ones.' He replied, 'Well done, good servant! You have been faithful in
15 this very small matter; take charge of ten cities.' Then the second came and reported, 'Your gold coin, sir, has earned five more.' And to this servant
20 too he said, 'You, take charge of five cities.' Then the other servant came and said, 'Sir, here is your gold coin; I kept it stored away in a handkerchief, for I was
25 afraid of you, because you are a demanding person; you take up what you did not lay down and you harvest what you did not plant.' He said to him, 'With
30 your own words I shall condemn you, you wicked servant. You knew I was a demanding person, taking up what I did not lay down and harvesting what I
35 did not plant; why did you not put my money in a bank? Then on my return I would have collected it with interest.' And to those standing by he said, 'Take
40 the gold coin from him and give it to the servant who has ten.' But they said to him, 'Sir, he has

to whom much is given, much will be required.

When Jesus relates that the gold of the one who did nothing with

ten gold coins.' 'I tell you, to everyone who has, more will be given, but from the one who has not, even what he has will be taken away. Now as for those enemies of mine who did not want me as their king, bring them here and slay them before me.' (12 – 27)

I tell you, if they keep silent, the stones will cry out!...If this day you only knew what makes for peace -- but now it is hidden from your eyes. For the days are coming upon you when your enemies will raise a palisade against you; they will encircle you and hem you in on all sides. They will smash you to the ground and your children within you, and they will not leave one stone upon another within you because you did not recognize the time of your visitation. (40 – 44)

It is written, 'My house shall be a house of prayer, but you have made it a den of thieves.' (46)

Chapter 20

[A] man planted a vineyard, leased it to tenant farmers, and then went on a journey for a long time. At harvest time he sent a servant to the tenant farmers to receive some of the produce of the vineyard. But they beat the servant and sent

it was to be given to the one with the ten pieces, there was a negative response on the part of the listeners. Jesus defended the action. It is to be a reward for the greatness of the enthusiasm in the one who exerted the most.

Years ahead, Jesus prophesied the destruction of Jerusalem. It was and continues to be a love affair between Himself and this city. As He prophesied, so did history record that it happened just as He said it would.

The justifiable anger of Jesus in the temple teaches the disciple how important it is to God for all to maintain reverence in holy places.

This parable depicts the truth of what Jesus knew about what the future had in store for Him. It would seem that the people who heard what He was saying would read between the lines, but they did not. This is just one more parable that Jesus presented,

him away empty-handed. So he proceeded to send another servant, but him also they beat and insulted and sent away empty-handed. Then he proceeded to send a third, but this one too they wounded and threw out. The owner of the vineyard said, 'What shall I do? I shall send my beloved son; maybe they will respect him.' But when the tenant farmers saw him they said to one another, 'This is the heir. Let us kill him that the inheritance may become ours.' So they threw him out of the vineyard and killed him. What will the owner of the vineyard do to them? He will come and put those tenant farmers to death and turn over the vineyard to others. (9 – 16)

hoping to wake the people up and bring them to their senses as to Who He really was. Then, as today, they were so filled with their own thoughts that they were not eager to introduce new, and never before brought out, thoughts into their minds.

What then does this scripture passage mean: / 'The stone which the builders rejected / has become the cornerstone'? / Everyone who falls on that stone will be dashed to pieces; and it will crush anyone on whom it falls. (17 – 18)

Jesus points out in His own unique way that He is the corner stone, and His teachings will have the power to crush those who do not take them to heart.

Then repay to Caesar what belongs to Caesar and to God what belongs to God. (25)

Church and State could live in harmony if each person gives to each what is due.

The children of this age marry and remarry; but those who are deemed worthy to attain to the coming age and to the resurrection of the dead neither marry nor are given in marriage. They

We are given another inkling as to what the future will be like. There will be no marriage, that is, the number of human persons will reach the point designated by the Creator.

can no longer die, for they are like angels; and they are the children of God because they are the ones who will rise. That the dead will rise even Moses made known in the passage about the bush, when he called 'Lord' the God of Abraham, the God of Isaac, and the God of Jacob; and he is not God of the dead, but of the living, for to him all are alive. (34 – 38)

Humans will be like angels on the other side of what is known as the resurrection of the dead.

How do they claim that the Messiah is the Son of David? For David himself in the Book of Psalms says: / 'The Lord said to my lord, / "Sit at my right hand till / I make your enemies your footstool." '/ Now if David calls him 'lord,' how can he be his son? (41 – 44)

This is one more time when Jesus takes the opportunity to challenge the Pharisees and the Scribes. To understand the proper words of the psalm one must be a believer. Through faith, the mind is opened and is capable of a deeper understanding, one assisted by the spirit.

Be on guard against the scribes, who like to go around in long robes and love greetings in marketplaces, seats of honor in synagogues, and places of honor at banquets. They devour the houses of widows and, as a pretext, recite lengthy prayers. They will receive a very severe condemnation. (46 – 47)

It was statements like this that angered the Scribes and Pharisees and finally aroused in them such hatred and the desire of revenge that they finally were the instruments of His being put to death. One thing is sure, Jesus did not fall victim to what is known today as 'political correctness.'

Chapter 21

I tell you truly, this poor widow put in more than all the rest; for those others have all made offerings from their surplus wealth, but she, from her poverty, has offered her whole

There are degrees of sacrifice and generosity. Jesus knew experientially the depth and height of sacrifice and generosity in giving Himself to be put to death for the salvation of mankind.

livelihood. (3 – 4)

All that you see here -- the days will come when there will not be left a stone upon another stone that will not be thrown down....See that you not be deceived, for many will come in my name, saying, 'I am he,' and 'The time has come.' Do not follow them! When you hear of wars and insurrections, do not be terrified; for such things must happen first, but it will not immediately be the end....Nation will rise against nation, and kingdom against kingdom. There will be powerful earthquakes, famines, and plagues from place to place; and awesome sights and mighty signs will come from the sky.

(6 – 11)

Once again Jesus is reminding His listeners that Jerusalem will be destroyed. He speaks of the end times and is reassuring in that His followers need not fear, but they must be wise not to be led astray by those who are not of God. Jesus gives somewhat of a time table as to the chronological sequence of what is sure to take place. It is interesting that He speaks of mighty signs from the sky. We hear much of these same predictions in our day.

Before all this happens, however, they will seize and persecute you, they will hand you over to the synagogues and to prisons, and they will have you led before kings and governors because of my name. It will lead to your giving testimony. Remember, you are not to prepare your defense beforehand, for I myself shall give you a wisdom in speaking that all your adversaries will be powerless to resist or refute. You will even be handed over by parents, brothers, relatives, and friends, and they will put some of you to death. You will be hated by all

Though there are many dangers that must befall the disciples, Jesus is reassuring that they need not even begin to think of their own defense. He promises to give them responses of divine wisdom confounding their adversaries.

because of my name, but not a hair on your head will be destroyed. By your perseverance you will secure your lives.

When you see Jerusalem surrounded by armies, know that its desolation is at hand. Then those in Judea must flee to the mountains. Let those within the city escape from it, and let those in the countryside not enter the city, for these days are the time of punishment when all the scriptures are fulfilled. Woe to pregnant women and nursing mothers in those days, for a terrible calamity will come upon the earth and a wrathful judgment upon this people. They will fall by the edge of the sword and be taken as captives to all the Gentiles; and Jerusalem will be trampled underfoot by the Gentiles until the times of the Gentiles are fulfilled. (12 – 24)

There will be signs in the sun, the moon, and the stars, and on earth nations will be in dismay, perplexed by the roaring of the sea and the waves. People will die of fright in anticipation of what is coming upon the world, for the powers of the heavens will be shaken. And then they will see the Son of Man coming in a cloud with power and great glory. But when these signs begin to happen, stand erect and raise your heads because your redemption is at hand. (25 – 28)

One must believe that Jesus gives all of these warnings in love, being genuinely concerned for those who give witness to His name, to His teaching. We know that in the past, Jerusalem had been destroyed, and yet, there are those who would do the same in our own day.

Many of the things that Jesus speaks of here have never happened in history. One can conclude that they are still to transpire. We know that God does not wish to be served in fear, nonetheless, the horrible things He is speaking of, by His own words, will happen. Without doubt his enemies are asking for trouble because of lack of morality in our own day. In conclusion, He gives the final happening, one that is of hope, one in which He speaks of redemption.

Consider the fig tree and all the other trees. When their buds burst open, you see for yourselves and know that summer is
5 now near; in the same way, when you see these things happening, know that the kingdom of God is near. Amen, I say to you, this generation will not pass
10 away until all these things have taken place. Heaven and earth will pass away, but my words will not pass away. (29 – 33)

His disciples of all ages have been aware of these warnings. He is intent on speaking for the purpose of informing and preparing those of whatever age He makes reference to. He does give clues. He does not give dates.

15 Beware that your hearts do not become drowsy from carousing and drunkenness and the anxieties of daily life, and that day catch you by surprise
20 like a trap. For that day will assault everyone who lives on the face of the earth. Be vigilant at all times and pray that you have the strength to escape the tribu-
25 lations that are imminent and to stand before the Son of Man. (34 – 36)

This prophecy is exactly what is being offered by many individuals in our day. In the shortest presentation of what will happen in the End Days, everything is covered as to the behavior of Jesus' disciples IN OUR PRESENT DAY! The Key Words are: "Beware that your hearts do not become drowsy..." and "Be vigilant at all times and pray for the strength..."

Chapter 22

30
This is my body, which will be given for you; do this in memory of me....This cup is the new covenant in my blood,
35 which will be shed for you. (19 –20)

Herein is instituted the Eucharist, the Central Dogma Of Our Faith.

For the Son of Man indeed goes as it has been determined;
40 but woe to that man by whom he is betrayed. (22)

The kings of the Gentiles lord it over them and those in authority over them are addressed as 'Benefactors'; but among you it shall not be so. Rather, let the greatest among you be as the youngest, and the leader as the servant. For who is greater: the one seated at table or the one who serves? Is it not the one seated at table? I am among you as the one who serves. It is you who have stood by me in my trials; and I confer a kingdom on you, just as my Father has conferred one on me, that you may eat and drink at my table in my kingdom; and you will sit on thrones judging the twelve tribes of Israel. (25 – 30)

Simon, Simon, behold Satan has demanded to sift all of you like wheat, but I have prayed that your own faith may not fail; and once you have turned back, you must strengthen your brothers. (31 – 32)

When I sent you forth without a moneybag or a sack or sandals, were you in need of anything? (35)

But now one who has a moneybag should take it, and likewise a sack, and one who does not have a sword should sell his cloak and buy one. For I tell you that this scripture must be fulfilled in me, namely, 'He was counted among the wicked;'

These words are parting words to the Apostles, but they fit today for today's disciples.

The disciples of Jesus of all centuries were and are to continue to be servants to others, lowly, childlike, and loving. As the Apostles were formed by the Holy Spirit, so the same Holy Spirit has formed and continues to form disciples in every century to carry on the work of the Apostles, the work that Jesus assigned to them and through them to every single disciple till the end of time.

The disciple is to be under the care and under the authority of the successor of St. Peter and receive strength through him. One is reminded here of the primacy that Jesus gave to Peter.

and indeed what is written about me is coming to fulfillment. (36 – 37)

5   Pray that you may not undergo the test. (40)

Father, if you are willing, take this cup away from me; still, not
10   my will but yours be done.
(42)

Why are you sleeping? Get up and pray that you may not un-
15   dergo the test. (46)

These words addressed to the three Apostles can be taken seriously by each disciple.

Have you come out as against a robber, with swords and clubs? Day after day I was with you in
20   the temple area, and you did not seize me; but this is your hour, the time for the power of darkness. (52 - 53)

25   **Chapter 23**

Daughters of Jerusalem, do not weep for me; weep instead for yourselves and for your chil-
30   dren, for indeed, the days are coming when people will say, 'Blessed are the barren, the wombs that never bore and the breasts that never nursed.' At
35   that time people will say to the mountains, 'Fall upon us!' and to the hills, 'Cover us!' for if these things are done when the wood is green what will happen
40   when it is dry? (28 – 30)

Even in the state of great suffering, Jesus is giving a special teaching to the women weeping for Him.

A prophecy for our day given almost two thousand years ago.

Father, forgive them; they

While hanging on the cross

know not what they do. (34)

Chapter 24

These are my words that I spoke to you while I was still with you, that everything written about me in the Law of Moses and in the prophets and psalms must be fulfilled. (44)

Thus it is written that the Messiah would suffer and rise from the dead on the third day and that repentance, for the forgiveness of sins, would be preached in his name to all the nations, beginning from Jerusalem. You are witnesses of these things. And [behold] I am sending the promise of my Father upon you; but stay in the city until you are clothed with power from on high. (46 – 49)

Jesus gives the example to the disciple always to be forgiving.

Jesus with these words had commissioned the Apostles to go forth to preach and do as He did. They were to await the coming of the Holy Spirit after which they were to go out into the world to preach the Good News. The disciple has a similar responsibility always under the direction and authority of the Successor of St. Peter and under the guidance of his bishop, prompted and nudged by the Holy Spirit.

Notes

Notes

Searching Through the Teachings of Jesus - - -

As Found in the Gospel of St. John

So as to Implant Them into Your Heart

Chapter 1

"Do you believe because I told you that I saw you under the fig tree? You will see greater things than this." And he said to him, "Amen, amen, I say to you, you will see the sky opened and the angels of God ascending and descending on the Son of Man." (50 – 51)

Chapter 2

Destroy this temple and in three days I will raise it up. (19)

Chapter 3

Amen, amen, I say to you, no one can see the kingdom of God without being born from above. (3)

Amen, amen, I say to you, no one can enter the kingdom of God without being born of water and Spirit. What is born of flesh is flesh and what is born of spirit is spirit. Do not be amazed that I told you, 'You must be born from above.' The wind blows where it wills, and you can hear the sound it makes, but you do not know where it comes from or where it goes; so it is with everyone who is born of the Spirit. (5 – 8)

You are the teacher of Israel and you do not understand this? Amen, amen, I say to you, we

"You must be born from above."

speak of what we know and we testify to what we have seen, but you people do not accept our testimony. If I tell you about
5 earthly things and you do not believe, how will you believe if I tell you about heavenly things? No one has gone up to heaven except the one who has come
10 down from heaven, the Son of Man. And just as Moses lifted up the serpent in the desert, so must the Son of Man be lifted up, so that everyone who be-
15 lieves in him may have eternal life. (10 – 15)

For God so loved the world that he gave his only Son, so that
20 everyone who believes in him might not perish but might have eternal life. For God did not send his Son into the world to condemn the world, but that the
25 world might be saved through him. Whoever believes in him will not be condemned, but whoever does not believe has already been condemned, be-
30 cause he has not believed in the name of the only Son of God. And this is the verdict, that the light came into the world, but people preferred darkness to
35 light, because their works were evil. For everyone who does wicked things hates the light and does not come toward the light, so that his works might
40 not be exposed. But whoever lives the truth comes to the light, so that his works may be

"Whoever believes in him will not be condemned, but whoever does not believe already has been condemned, because he has not believed in the name of the only Son of God."

clearly seen as done in God.
(16 – 21)

The one who comes from above is above all. The one who is of the earth is earthly and speaks of earthly things. But the one who comes from heaven [is above all]. He testifies to what he has seen and heard, but no one accepts his testimony. Whoever does accept his testimony certifies that God is trustworthy. For the one whom God sent speaks the words of God. He does not ration his gift of the Spirit. The Father loves the Son and has given everything over to him. Whoever believes in the Son has eternal life, but whoever disobeys the Son will not see life, but the wrath of God remains upon him. (31 – 36)

Accept the testimony of Jesus.

Believe in Jesus.

Chapter 4

If you knew the gift of God and who is saying to you, 'Give me a drink,' you would have asked him and he would have given you living water....Everyone who drinks this water will be thirsty again; but whoever drinks the water I shall give will never thirst; the water I shall give will become in him a spring of water welling up to eternal life....Believe me, woman, the hour is coming when you will worship the Father neither on this mountain nor in Jerusalem. You people

Whoever drinks of the water of truth that comes forth from Jesus will never be thirsty.

worship what you do not understand; we worship what we understand, because salvation is from the Jews. But the hour is
5 coming, and is now here, when true worshipers will worship the Father in Spirit and truth; and indeed the Father seeks such people to worship him. God is
10 Spirit, and those who worship him must worship in Spirit and truth. (10 – 24)

"God is Spirit, and those who worship him must worship in Spirit and truth."

My food is to do the will of
15 the one who sent me and to finish his work. Do you not say, 'In four months the harvest will be here?' I tell you, look up and see the fields ripe for the harvest.
20 The reaper is already receiving his payment and gathering crops for eternal life, so that the sower and reaper can rejoice together. For here the saying is verified
25 that 'One sows and another reaps.' I sent you to reap what you have not worked for; others have done the work, and you are sharing the fruits of their
30 work. (34 – 38)

The primary purpose of Jesus' coming onto earth was to do exactly what the Father wanted Him to do. He did not come to do what His will was, but that which was willed by the Father.

Unless you people see signs and wonders, you will not believe. (48)

35

Chapter 5

My Father is at work until now, so I am at work. (17)

40

Amen, amen, I say to you, a son cannot do anything on his

own, but only what he sees his father doing; for what he does, his son will do also. For the Father loves his Son and shows him everything that he himself does, and he will show him greater works than these, so that you may be amazed. For just as the Father raises the dead and gives life, so also does the Son give life to whomever he wishes. Nor does the Father judge anyone, but he has given all judgment to his Son, so that all may honor the Son just as they honor the Father. Whoever does not honor the Son does not honor the Father who sent him.

(19 – 23)

Amen, amen, I say to you, whoever hears my word and believes in the one who sent me has eternal life and will not come to condemnation, but has passed from death to life. Amen, amen, I say to you, the hour is coming and is now here when the dead will hear the voice of the Son of God, and those who hear will live. For just as the Father has life in himself, so also he gave his Son the possession of life in himself. And he gave him power to exercise judgment, because he is the Son of Man. Do not be amazed at this, because the hour is coming in which all who are in the tombs will hear his voice and will come out, those who have done good deeds to the resurrection of life,

The Father does not judge anyone. He has turned all judgments to Jesus, His Son.

"Whoever does not honor the Son does not honor the Father Who sent Him."

Eternal life will be given to those who believe in what Jesus teaches and who acknowledge that He has come forth from the Father.

Those who follow through on the words of Jesus will live, that is, will establish their abode in heaven for all eternity and enjoy the fullness of life, eternal joy.

At the command of Jesus, at a given time, all will rise in a resurrection from their tombs and will be judged worthy of reward

but those who have done wicked deeds to the resurrection of condemnation.

I cannot do anything on my own; I judge as I hear, and my judgment is just, because I do not seek my own will but the will of the one who sent me.

If I testify on my own behalf, my testimony cannot be verified. But there is another who testifies on my behalf, and I know that the testimony he gives on my behalf is true. You sent emissaries to John, and he testified to the truth. I do not accept testimony from a human being, but I say this so that you may be saved. He was a burning and shining lamp, and for a while you were content to rejoice in his light. But I have testimony greater than John's. The works that the Father gave me to accomplish, these works that I perform testify on my behalf that the Father has sent me. Moreover, the Father who sent me has testified on my behalf. But you have never heard his voice nor seen his form, and you do not have his word remaining in you, because you do not believe in the one whom he has sent. You search the scriptures, because you think you have eternal life through them; even they testify on my behalf. But you do not want to come to me to have life. (24 – 40)

I do not accept human praise;

for their goodness or worthy of punishment because of their evil.

The Father gives testimony on behalf of His Son by the works that He does through Him.

The Sacred Scriptures testify on Jesus' behalf.

moreover, I know that you do not have the love of God in you. I came in the name of my Father, but you do not accept me; yet if another comes in his own name, you will accept him. How can you believe, when you accept praise from one another and do not seek the praise that comes from the only God? Do not think that I will accuse you before the Father: the one who will accuse you is Moses, in whom you have placed your hope. For if you had believed Moses, you would have believed me, because he wrote about me. But if you do not believe his writings, how will you believe my words? (41 – 47)

To accept praise from others is one thing, but more important is to accept the praise that comes from the Father.

Chapter 6

Amen, amen, I say to you, you are looking for me not because you saw signs but because you ate the loaves and were filled. Do not work for food that perishes but for the food that endures for eternal life, which the Son of Man will give you. For on him the Father, God, has set his seal.... This is the work of God, that you believe in the one he sent. (26 – 29)

Greater emphasis in life must be put on the food that Jesus gives to the soul, namely his presentation of truth and goodness as it comes forth from His own Person.

Amen, amen, I say to you, it was not Moses who gave the bread from heaven; my Father gives you the true bread from heaven. For the bread of God is that which comes down from

heaven and gives life to the world....I am the bread of life; whoever come to me will never hunger, and whoever believes in
5 me will never thirst. But I told you that although you have seen [me], you do not believe. Everything that the Father gives me will come to me, and I will not
10 reject anyone who comes to me, because I came down from heaven not to do my own will but the will of the one who sent me. And this is the will of the
15 one who sent me, that I should not lose anything of what he gave me, but that I should raise it [on] the last day. For this is the will of my Father, that ev-
20 eryone who sees the Son and believes in him may have eternal life, and I shall raise him [on] the last day. (32 – 40)

25 Stop murmuring among yourselves. No one can come to me unless the Father who sent me draw him, and I will raise him on the last day. It is written
30 in the prophets: / 'They shall all be taught by God.' / Everyone who listens to my Father and learns from him comes to me. Not that anyone has seen the
35 Father except the one who is from God; he has seen the Father. Amen, amen, I say to you, whoever believes has eternal life. I am the bread of life. Your an-
40 cestors ate the manna in the desert, but they died; this is the bread that comes down from

Jesus is the source of true spiritual life. Whoever comes to Him and accepts what He offers will never experience hunger or thirst. The hunger and thirst of the soul can be satisfied only by the life that He offers.

The Father and Jesus are one. The Father's will is that everyone who accepts His Son, believes in Him and follows through on His teaching will be raised to glory on the last day.

The nature of life that Jesus offers is a spiritual life, a life which will merit one's eternal salvation. He speaks of Himself as the Bread of Life. This is the way in which He is received in Holy Communion.

This also can be looked at as

heaven so that one may eat it and not die. I am the living bread that came down from heaven; whoever eats this bread will live forever; and the bread that I will give is my flesh for the life of the world. (43 – 51)

Amen, amen, I say to you, unless you eat the flesh of the Son of Man and drink his blood, you do not have life within you. Whoever eats my flesh and drinks my blood has eternal life, and I will raise him on the last day. For my flesh is true food, and my blood is true drink. Whoever eats my flesh and drinks my blood remains in me and I in him. Just as the living Father sent me and I have life because of the Father, so also the one who feeds on me will have life because of me. This is the bread that came down from heaven. Unlike your ancestors who ate and still died, whoever eats this bread will live forever. (53 – 58)

Does this shock you? What if you were to see the Son of Man ascending to where he was before? It is the spirit that gives life, while the flesh is of no avail. The words I have spoken to you are spirit and life. But there are some of you who do not believe….For this reason I have told you that no one can come to me unless it is granted him by my Father. (61 – 65)

Jesus giving Himself in death on the cross in order that human beings could have true life enjoying eternal bliss.

It is clear that Jesus insists that unless we eat His flesh and drink His blood, we cannot enter into eternal life in heaven. The prerequisite is belief in what He says to the degree of following through on actually receiving Him in Holy Communion. Jesus here speaks of the intimacy that results in receiving Him in the Eucharist. He makes it clear that a true intimacy is possible between Him and the soul who believes in Him and receives His Body and Blood in the Eucharist.

The flesh and blood He speaks of is to be taken in a spiritual way. It is the Gift of Himself that He gives to the human person in exchange for the gift of self of the human person in return.

Chapter 7

My time is not yet here, but the time is always right for you.
5 The world cannot hate you, but it hates me, because I testify to it that its works are evil. You go up to the feast. I am not going up to this feast, because my time
10 has not yet been fulfilled.

(6 – 8)

My teaching is not my own but is from the one who sent
15 me. Whoever chooses to do his will shall know whether my teaching is from God or whether I speak on my own. Whoever speaks on his own seeks his own
20 glory, but whoever seeks the glory of the one who sent him is truthful, and there is no wrong in him. Did not Moses give you the law? Yet none of
25 you keeps the law. Why are you trying to kill me?...I performed one work and all of you are amazed because of it. Moses gave you circumcision -- not
30 that it came from Moses but rather from the patriarchs -- and you circumcise a man on the sabbath. If a man can receive circumcision on a sabbath so that
35 the Law of Moses may not be broken, are you angry with me because I made a whole person well on a sabbath? Stop judging by appearances, but judge justly.
40

(16 – 24)

You know me and also know

The teaching that Jesus gives is that of the Father. Over and over again Jesus repeats this because He realizes that the multitude is slow in believing what He is offering. He is not saying anything on His own, but only that which the Father has Him speak.

Jesus maintains His right to cure on the Sabbath because He is the "Lord of the Sabbath".

Stop judging by appearances, judge by justice.

where I am from. Yet I did not come on my own, but the one who sent me, whom you do not know, is true. I know him, because I am from him, and he sent me. (28 – 29)

I will be with you only a little while longer, and then I will go to the one who sent me. You will look for me but not find [me], and where I am you cannot come. (33 – 34)

Let anyone who thirsts come to me and drink. Whoever believes in me, as scripture says: 'Rivers of living water will flow from within him.' (37 – 38)

Chapter 8

Let the one among you who is without sin be the first to throw a stone at her...Woman, where are they? Has no one condemned you?...Neither do I condemn you. Go, [and] from now on do not sin any more. (7 – 11)

I am the light of the world. Whoever follows me will not walk in darkness, but will have the light of life. (12)

Even if I do testify on my own behalf, my testimony can be verified, because I know where I came from and where I am going. But you do not know where I come from or where I

If we accept the life that Jesus wishes to give, we can share in a life that is divine. From within our person will pour out words of wisdom and acts of divine love.

Through a life with Jesus, one can radiate a confidence in traveling one's journey with a clarity of purpose.

The dialogue between the leaders of the people and Jesus

5

10

15

20

25

30

35

40

am going. You judge by appearances, but I do not judge anyone. And even if I should judge, my judgment is valid, because I am not alone, but it is I and the Father who sent me. Even in your law it is written that the testimony of two men can be verified. I testify on my behalf and so does the Father who sent me. (14 – 18)

You know neither me nor my Father. If you knew me, you would know my Father also. (19)

I am going away and you will look for me, but you will die in your sin. Where I am going you cannot come. (21)

You belong to what is below; I belong to what is above. You belong to this world, but I do not belong to this world. That is why I told you that you will die in your sins. For if you do not believe that I AM, you will die in your sins. (23 – 24)

What I told you from the beginning. I have much to say about you in condemnation. But the one who sent me is true, and what I heard from him I tell the world....When you lift up the Son of Man, then you will realize that I AM, and that I do nothing on my own, but I say only what the Father taught me. (25 – 28)

continues. He takes them to task for their blindness and for their inability to accept Him for Who He really is.

Jesus speaks clearly of Who He really is, and speaks with authority that if He is not accepted as He presents Himself, loss of salvation will be the consequence.

The one who sent me is with me. He has not left me alone, because I always do what is pleasing to him. (29)

If you remain in my word, you will truly be my disciples, and you will know the truth, and the truth will set you free. (31 – 32)

If one does what Jesus asks, the result in one's life will be that of experiencing the fullness of inner freedom.

Amen, amen, I say to you, everyone who commits sin is a slave of sin. A slave does not remain in a household forever, but a son always remains. So if a son frees you, then you will truly be free. I know that you are descendants of Abraham. But you are trying to kill me, because my word has no room among you. I tell you what I have seen in the Father's presence; then do what you have heard from the Father. (34 – 38)

If you were Abraham's children, you would be doing the works of Abraham. But now you are trying to kill me, a man who has told you the truth that I heard from God; Abraham did not do this. You are doing the works of your father!
(39 – 41)

If God were your Father, you would love me, for I came from God and am here; I did not come on my own, but he sent me. Why do you not understand what I am saying? Because you cannot bear to hear my

word. You belong to your father
the devil and you willingly carry
out your father's desires. He was
a murderer from the beginning
5 and does not stand in truth, because there is no truth in him.
When he tells a lie, he speaks in
character, because he is a liar and
the father of lies. But because I
10 speak the truth, you do not believe me. Can any of you charge
me with sin? If I am telling the
truth, why do you not believe
me? Whoever belongs to God
15 hears the words of God; for this
reason you do not listen, because
you do not belong to God.
(42 – 47)

Jesus pleads to be accepted for
Who He is. He comes up con-
tinuously with opposition from
leadership. He minces no words
telling it how it is. It was pre-
cisely because He was honest
and outspoken that these same
leaders were instrumental in His
being put to death.

20   I am not possessed; I honor
my Father, but you dishonor
me. I do not seek my own glory;
there is one who seeks it and he
is the one who judges. Amen,
25 amen, I say to you, whoever
keeps my word will never see
death. (49 – 51)

Jesus' words give life to the soul.
He knows what will make it
possible for human beings to
experience the fullness of life.
He shares this knowledge lovingly, but with authority.

If I glorify myself, my glory is
30 worth nothing; but it is my Father who glorifies me, of whom
you say, 'He is our God'. You
do not know him, but I know
him. And if I should say that
35 I do not know him, I would be
like you a liar. But I do know
him and I keep his word.
Abraham your father rejoiced to
see my day; he saw it and was
40 glad. (54 – 56)

Amen, amen, I say to you,

before Abraham came to be I
AM. (58)

Chapter 9

Neither he nor his parents
sinned; it is so that the works of
God might be made visible
through him. We have to do the
works of the one who sent me
while it is day. Night is coming
when no one can work. While I
am in the world, I am the light
of the world. (3 – 5)

Physical disabilities are not the
result of personal sin, but rather
that God's plan might be fulfilled through them. Through
them God is able to give blessings which are more spiritually
fruitful.

I came into this world for
judgment, so that those who do
not see might see, and those
who do see might become
blind....If you were blind, you
would have no sin; but now you
are saying, 'We see', so your sin
remains. (39 – 41)

Jesus' teachings dispel ignorance
and make one responsible for
his/her actions.

Chapter 10

Amen, amen, I say to you,
whoever does not enter a
sheepfold through the gate but
climbs over elsewhere is a thief
and a robber. But whoever
enters through the gate is the
shepherd of the sheep. The
gatekeeper opens it for him, and
the sheep hear his voice, as he
calls his own sheep by name and
leads them out. When he has
driven out all his own, he walks
ahead of them, and the sheep
follow him, because they recognize his voice. But they will not
follow a stranger; they will run

Once a relationship with Jesus
is entered into, an individual
experiences a confidence in living, following Jesus in trust and
without hesitation.

away from him, because they do not recognize the voice of strangers. (1 - 5)

5   Amen, amen, I say to you, I am the gate for the sheep. All who came [before me] are thieves and robbers, but the sheep did not listen to them. I
10 am the gate. Whoever enters through me will be saved, and will come in and go out and find pasture. A thief comes only to steal and slaughter and destroy;
15 I came so that they might have life and have it more abundantly. I am the good shepherd. A good shepherd lays down his life for the sheep. A hired man,
20 who is not a shepherd and whose sheep are not his own, sees a wolf coming and leaves the sheep and runs away, and the wolf catches and scatters them.
25 This is because he works for pay and has no concern for the sheep. I am the good shepherd, and I know mine and mine know me, just as the Father
30 knows me and I know the Father; and I will lay down my life for the sheep. I have other sheep that do not belong to this fold. These also I must lead, and they
35 will hear my voice, and there will be one flock, one shepherd. This is why the Father loves me, because I lay down my life in order to take it up again. No one
40 takes it from me, but I lay it down on my own. I have power to lay it down, and power to take

It is not only through the teaching of Jesus that one experiences confidence on one's spiritual journey, but also through the goodness which He radiates. The loving and caring Jesus is the proof of the pudding wherein He practices what He preaches and preaches what He practices.

The gentleness of Jesus is reflected in considering Himself as a Shepherd. He is aware of this quality within Himself and presents Himself as the gentle Jesus. One can almost hear Him say it, "Learn from Me for I am meek and gentle of heart."

Jesus is a gentle lamb even when He is being led to the slaughter.

it up again. This command I have received from my Father.
(7 – 18)

I told you and you do not be-lieve me. The works I do in my Father's name testify to me. But you do not believe, because you are not among my sheep. My sheep hear my voice; I know them, and they follow me. I give them eternal life, and they shall never perish. No one can take them out of my hand. My Fa-ther, who has given them to me, is greater than all, and no one can take them out of the Father's hand. The Father and I are one.
(25 – 30)

I have shown you many good works from my Father. For which of these are you trying to stone me? (32)

Is it not written in your law, 'I said, "You are gods?"' If it calls them gods to whom the word of God came, and scripture can-not be set aside, can you say that the one whom the Father has consecrated and sent into the world blasphemes because I said, 'I am the Son of God?' If I do not perform my Father's works, do not believe me; but if I perform them, even if you do not believe me, believe the works, so that you may realize [and understand] that the Father is in me and I am in the Father.
(34 – 38)

The quality of gentleness is a must for anyone who wants to grasp the wishes of Jesus. One cannot learn to be gentle except by practicing gentleness. It is exactly through virtue that the soul is disposed to other virtues, disposed to received an abun-dance of grace.

A true follower of Jesus must expect unkind reactions from others just for trying to be more like Jesus.

There is a tremendous lesson here, namely that it is accept-able as a follower of Jesus to de-fend oneself when questioned about our behavior. Discern-ment is needed here as for in-stance, Jesus remained silent before Pilate.

Chapter 11

This illness is not to end in
death, but is for the glory of
God, that the Son of God may
be glorified through it. (4)

Are there not twelve hours in
a day? If one walks during the
day, he does not stumble, because he sees the light of this
world. But if one walks at night,
he stumbles, because the light
is not in him. (9 – 10)

When truth is what one lives by,
there is no need for confusion
(darkness), Jesus gives forth
truths which will stand firm in
every circumstance.

I am the resurrection and the
life; whoever believes in me,
even if he dies, will live, and everyone who lives and believes in
me will never die. Do you believe this? (25 – 26)

Jesus equates belief and life.
Believing in what Jesus teaches
puts the person on a higher level
of life, for what is believed
comes from a divine source.

Chapter 12

The hour has come for the
Son of Man to be glorified.
Amen, amen, I say to you, unless a grain of wheat falls to the
ground and dies, it remains just
a grain of wheat; but if it dies, it
produces much fruit. Whoever
loves his life loses it, and whoever hates his life in this world
will preserve it for eternal life.
(23 – 25)

Death to self, death to one's ego,
death to one's self centeredness,
makes it possible for the divine
life to enter into one, and cause
it to put one on a higher plane
of life than that which is offered
in the world.

Whoever serves me must follow me, and where I am, there
also will my servant be. The Father will honor whoever serves
me.
I am troubled now. Yet

To live by purpose, that is, to
do what it is that one has been
put into the world for. The Father Creator, as a responsible
Parent, had in mind certain spe-
cifics for each person created.

what should I say? 'Father, save me from this hour?' But it was for this purpose that I came to this hour. Father, glorify your name. (26 – 28)

The voice did not come for my sake but for yours. Now is the time of judgment on this world; now the ruler of this world will be driven out. And when I am lifted up from the earth, I will draw everyone to myself. (30 – 32)

The light will be among you only a little while. Walk while you have the light, so that darkness may not overcome you. Whoever walks in the dark does not know where he is going. While you have the light, believe in the light, so that you may become children of the light. (35 – 36)

Whoever believes in me believes not only in me but also in the one who sent me, and whoever sees me sees the one who sent me. I came into the world as light, so that everyone who believes in me might not remain in darkness. And if anyone hears my words and does not observe them, I do not condemn him, for I did not come to condemn the world but to save the world. Whoever rejects me and does not accept my words has something to judge him: the word that I spoke, it will condemn

With the help of mind and prayer, this purpose can be clarified.

5

Jesus' death frees the world of sin. He, as the Liberator, has within Himself a drawing power to those in the bonds of sin. As 10 the positive pole it attracts the negative and draws it to itself.

15

The words of Jesus give light. They bring a definite clarity to the meaning of life, its purpose, its goals, its crosses, its hopes and the like. Belief is essential, not 20 just the thought of belief, but the pure experience of belief that emanates from the will.

25

Who believes in Jesus believes also in the Father Who sent Him. He came for the purpose of giving light, clarity to life, a 30 fullness of meaning. Should one choose to walk in the dark, it is not Jesus Who will condemn him. To do this was not His purpose for coming. He came to 35 bring salvation to mankind. It will be nonetheless the very teaching of Jesus that will do the condemning, for it is also the teaching of the Father. 40

him on the last day, because I did not speak on my own, but the Father who sent me commanded me what to say and
5 speak. And I know that his commandment is eternal life. So what I say, I say as the Father told me. (44 – 50)

10 **Chapter 13**

Whoever has bathed has no need except to have his feet washed, for he is clean all over;
15 so you are clean, but not all. (10)

Do you realize what I have done for you? You call me 'teacher' and 'master', and
20 rightly so, for indeed I am. If I, therefore, the master and teacher, have washed your feet, you ought to wash one another's feet. I have given you a model
25 to follow, so that as I have done for you, you should also do. Amen, amen, I say to you, no slave is greater than his master nor any messenger greater than
30 the one who sent him. If you understand this, blessed are you if you do it. I am not speaking of all of you. I know those whom I have chosen. But so that
35 the scripture might be fulfilled, 'The one who ate my food has raised his heel against me.' From now on I am telling you before it happens, so that when it hap-
40 pens you may believe that I AM. Amen, amen, I say to you, whoever receives the one I send

In washing the feet of the Apostles, Jesus makes it known that He wishes His followers to act in the same way. His followers are humble themselves in providing for the needs of others. Jesus' demonstration of humility is to be a lesson to His followers how they are to treat each other.

Jesus teaches that it is not we who have chosen Him, but that He has chosen us. It is a reminder of His saying, "Many are called, but few are chosen."

receives me, and whoever receives me receives the one who sent me. (12 – 20)

Now is the Son of Man glorified, and God is glorified in him. [If God is glorified in him,] God will also glorify him in himself, and he will glorify him at once. My children, I will be with you only a little while longer. You will look for me, and as I told the Jews, 'Where I go you cannot come,' so now I say it to you, I give you a new commandment: love one another. As I have loved you, so you also should love one another. This is how all will know that you are my disciples, if you have love for one another. (31 – 35)

Chapter 14

Do not let your hearts be troubled. You have faith in God; have faith also in me. In my Father's house there are many dwelling places. If there were not, would I have told you that I am going to prepare a place for you? And if I go and prepare a place for you, I will come back again and take you to myself, so that where I am you also may be. Where [I] am going you know the way. (1 – 4)

I am the way and the truth and the life. No one comes to the Father except through me. If you know me, then you will

Jesus gives those who follow Him what He calls a "new commandment," simply because it differs from the commandment of the Old Testament. One is not to love in return for love, but to love one another as Jesus loved and loves, with a love that is deep enough and truly unconditional, so much so that one would readily die for another should this become necessary.

Jesus speaks lovingly to the Apostles and to each of His followers, reminding them that with faith in Him, there need be no fear. As He told them that He will be preparing a place for them and so for all of His faithful followers, He expresses a deep concern for all who have faith in Him.

In His expression, "I am the way and the truth and the life," He brings to the mind of each that there is no other way to attain

also know my Father. From now on you do know him and have seen him. (6 – 7)

5   Have I been with you for so long a time and you still do not know me, Philip? Whoever has seen me has seen the Father. How can you say, 'Show us the 10 Father?' Do you not believe that I am in the Father and the Father is in me? The words that I speak to you I do not speak on my own. The Father who dwells 15 in me is doing his works. Believe me that I am in the Father and the Father is in me, or else, believe because of the works themselves. Amen, amen, I say to 20 you, whoever believes in me will do the works that I do, and will do greater ones than these, because I am going to the Father. And whatever you ask in my 25 name, I will do, so that the Father may be glorified in the Son. If you ask anything of me in my name, I will do it. If you love me, you will keep my com- 30 mandments. And I will ask the Father, and he will give you another Advocate to be with you always, the Spirit of truth, which the world cannot accept, be- 35 cause it neither sees nor knows it. But you know it, because it remains with you, and will be in you. I will not leave you orphans; I will come to you. In a 40 little while the world will no longer see me, but you will see me, because I live and you will

the fullness of life except through Him.

As followers of Jesus, we must never forget that there is a real oneness between Jesus and the Father. "I am in the Father, the Father is in me."

Jesus is most generous in inviting His followers to make petitions to the Father. He promises that He Himself will intercede for those who ask. Surely, it is not that when one asks in His name, there is a guarantee of response and granting of a request. To ask in His name means that we would not ask for anything that He Himself would not ask for. If there is an obedience to His commandments and this, in love, He promises to send the Holy Spirit. The Holy Spirit has been sent.

Intimacy is once again offered here by Jesus to those who obey His commandments in love. His offer to reveal Himself to such is surely an offer which expresses the deep love that is His for those who give Him the recognition that He deserves.

live. On that day you will realize that I am in my Father and
you are in me and I in you.
Whoever has my command-
ments and observes them is the
one who loves me. And whoever
loves me will be loved by my
Father, and I will love him and
reveal myself to him. (9 – 21)

Whoever loves me will keep
my word, and my Father will
love him, and we will come to
him and make our dwelling
with him. Whoever does not
love me does not keep my
words; yet the word you hear is
not mine but that of the Father
who sent me.

I have told you this while I am
with you. The Advocate, the
holy Spirit that the Father will
send in my name -- he will teach
you everything and remind you
of all that [I] told you. (23 – 26)

Peace I leave with you; my
peace I give to you. Not as the
world gives do I give it to you.
Do not let your hearts be
troubled or afraid. You heard me
tell you, 'I am going away and I
will come back to you.' If you
loved me, you would rejoice
that I am going to the Father;
for the Father is greater than I.
And now I have told you this
before it happens, so that when
it happens you may believe. I
will no longer speak much with
you, for the ruler of the world is
coming. He has no power over

In addition to the offer of intimacy, there is added an offer of
an indwelling not only by Jesus
Himself, but by His Father as
well. The intimacy that is en-
joyed between the Father and
Jesus is offered freely to those
who believe in Him and believe
in the oneness that exists between the both of them. Here,
too, once again, there is an offer to send the Holy Spirit,
Who will teach and remind each
of all the truths Jesus taught.

Jesus leaves a great gift to His
followers, that of peace, not just
any peace, but the peace that He
enjoys within Himself.

After all is said and done, Jesus'
last will and testament is that of
giving His followers a peace that
can not be attained by one's own
human effort. It can not be
found in, or produced by, the
world. His chief request of His
followers is that they have trust
in Him and in the Father Who
sent Him into our midst. Jesus

me, but the world must know that I love the Father and that I do just as the Father has commanded me. Get up, let us go.
5 (27 – 31)

Chapter 15

I am the true vine, and my Fa-
10 ther is the vine grower. He takes away every branch in me that does not bear fruit, and everyone that does he prunes so that it bears more fruit. You are al-
15 ready pruned because of the word that I spoke to you. Remain in me, as I remain in you. Just as a branch cannot bear fruit on its own unless it remains on
20 the vine, so neither can you unless you remain in me. I am the vine, you are the branches. Whoever remains in me and I in him will bear much fruit, be-
25 cause without me you can do nothing. Anyone who does not remain in me will be thrown out like a branch and wither; people will gather them and throw
30 them into a fire and they will be burned. If you remain in me and my words remain in you, ask for whatever you want and it will be done for you. By this
35 is my Father glorified, that you bear much fruit and become my disciples. As the Father loves me, so I also love you. Remain in my love. If you keep my command-
40 ments, you will remain in my love, just as I have kept my Father's commandments and

points out Satan as the "ruler of the world". Neither at the time when He spoke nor now, has Satan any power over Him.

Jesus as the true vine is the source of all good. Our good actions must be connected to His Will. They are to be engaged in, not for our own personal benefit, but for the carrying out of His Divine Will.

Jesus speaks of the "pruning" that is carried out by His Father. By this is meant that the Father takes the initiative of keeping the followers of Jesus humble through suffering. At another time, He spoke of the cross, "Unless you pick up your cross daily, you cannot be my followers." It is by a willing and generous taking up of our daily responsibilities and hardships that we walk in His footsteps.

remain in his love. (1 – 10)

I have told you this so that my joy may be in you and your joy may be complete. This is my commandment: love one another as I love you. No one has greater love than this, to lay down one's life for one's friends. You are my friends if you do what I command you. I no longer call you slaves, because a slave does not know what his master is doing. I have called you friends, because I have told you everything I have heard from my Father. It was not you who chose me, but I who chose you and appointed you to go and bear fruit that will remain, so that whatever you ask the Father in my name he may give you. (11 – 16)

This I command you: love one another. If the world hates you, realize that it hated me first. If you belonged to the world, the world would love its own; but because you do not belong to the world, and I have chosen you out of the world, the world hates you. Remember the word I spoke to you, 'No slave is greater than his master.' If they persecuted me, they will also persecute you. If they kept my word, they will also keep yours. And they will do all these things to you on account of my name, because they do not know the one who sent me. If I had not

5

Peace and joy go hand in hand. As Jesus leaves us His peace, He also wishes us to be a sharer of the joy that is His. This is living proof that we are followers of 10 Jesus when our heart is filled with joy despite our living in this "vale of tears."

15

Jesus shares with us all that He has received from the Father. This gives clear evidence to His 20 depth of love for those whom He has chosen to be His followers.

Over and over again He repeats 25 His command to His followers, that they love each other.

Jesus expresses the wish that we 30 accept the hardships which the world presses upon us because the world had treated Him in exactly the same way. We should not expect anything different. 35 On the other hand, as there were those who accepted Jesus, listened to Him and believed Him, there will be those who will listen to and believe in His 40 followers.

come and spoken to them, they would have no sin; but as it is they have no excuse for their sin. Whoever hates me also hates my
5 Father. If I had not done works among them that no one else ever did, they would not have sin; but as it is, they have seen and hated both me and my Fa-
10 ther. But in order that the word written in their law might be fulfilled, 'They hated me without cause.' (17 – 25)

Followers of Jesus must expect to be hated in the world as Jesus Himself was hated, and this without cause, since He did nothing but that which was good and loving.

15   When the Advocate comes whom I will send you from the Father, the Spirit of truth that proceeds from the Father, he will testify to me. And you also tes-
20 tify, because you have been with me from the beginning.
(26 – 27)

Chapter 16

25
I have told you this so that you may not fall away. They will ex-pel you from the synagogues; in fact, the hour is coming when
30 everyone who kills you will think he is offering worship to God. They will do this because they have not known either the Father or me. I have told you
35 this so that when their hour comes you may remember that I told you.
I did not tell you this from the beginning, because I was with
40 you. But now I am going to the one who sent me, and not one of you asks me, 'Where are you

These remarks are directed to the Apostles, but also to us in our present day. The early days of the Church when the Old Testament and the New Testament were both in transition, one leaving the present, the other entering into the present, is the same as it is today. We are leaving the New and entering

going?' But because I told you this, grief has filled your hearts. But I tell you the truth, it is better for you that I go. For if I do not go, the Advocate will not come to you. But if I go, I will send him to you. And when he comes he will convict the world in regard to sin and righteousness and condemnation: sin, because they do not believe in me; righteousness, because I am going to the Father and you will no longer see me; condemnation, because the ruler of this world has been condemned.

I have much more to tell you, but you cannot bear it now. But when he comes, the Spirit of truth, he will guide you to all truth. He will not speak on his own, but he will speak what he hears, and will declare to you the things that are coming. He will glorify me, because he will take from what is mine and declare it to you. Everything that the Father has is mine; for this reason I told you that he will take from what is mine and declare it to you. (1 – 15)

A little while and you will no longer see me, and again a little while later you will see me. (16)

Amen, amen, I say to you, you will weep and mourn, while the world rejoices; you will grieve, but your grief will become joy. When a woman is in labor, she is in anguish because her hour

into an era which will be upgraded to the New Testament. Nonetheless, the persecutions of old are intensifying in the present day.   5

Jesus reassures the Apostles telling them not to fear that He will always be with them. It is the same in our present day. No   10 need to be dominated by fear. Jesus is the same yesterday, today, and forever.

He sent the Holy Spirit not only   15 for their benefit, but for ours as well. As followers of Jesus, we have merited for ourselves, because of His suffering and death, an Advocate, the Holy Spirit,   20 Who has been within each of us since Baptism. He resides with us with His Gifts, with His Truth, With His Love ...

                              25

                              30

                              35

Jesus forewarns His Apostles, and through them each one of us, that due to the fact that we are His followers, there will be   40 weeping and grief, but that we are not to become saddened.

has arrived; but when she has given birth to a child, she no longer remembers the pain because of her joy that a child has
5 been born into the world. So you also are now in anguish. But I will see you again, and your hearts will rejoice, and no one will take your joy away from
10 you. On that day you will not question me about anything.
(20 – 23)

Amen, amen, I say to you,
15 whatever you ask the Father in my name he will give you. Until now you have not asked anything in my name; ask and you will receive, so that your joy may
20 be complete.

I have told you this in figures of speech. The hour is coming when I will no longer speak to you in figures but I will tell you
25 clearly about the Father. On that day you will ask in my name, and I do not tell you that I will ask the Father for you. For the Father himself loves you, be-
30 cause you have loved me and have come to believe that I came from God. I came from the Father and have come into the world. Now I am leaving the
35 world and going back to the Father. (23 – 28)

Do you believe now? Behold, the hour is coming and has ar-
40 rived when each of you will be scattered to his own home and you will leave me alone. But I

Our sadness will be turned to joy.

Jesus gives His followers easy access to the Father. Whatever we are to ask the Father for, it is to be done in the name of Jesus.

The Father, however, will answer prayers of the followers of Jesus simply because they have a love for His Son, and these requests may be made directly to the Father without leaning on Jesus.

Jesus spoke making use of parables during His stay among men; now that the Father has sent the Holy Spirit, it will be the Spirit Who will remind the followers of Jesus, of all that Jesus taught and they will be able to understand clearly all the wishes of Jesus.

The followers of Jesus are promised that they will have troubles in the world, but not to fear because Jesus has overpowered the world.

am not alone, because the Father is with me. I have told you this so that you might have peace in me. In the world you will have trouble, but take courage, I have conquered the world.
(31 – 33)

Chapter 17

Father, the hour has come. Give glory to your son, so that your son may glorify you, just as you gave him authority over all people, so that he may give eternal life to all you gave him. Now this is eternal life, that they should know you, the only true God, and the one whom you sent, Jesus Christ. I glorified you on earth by accomplishing the work that you gave me to do. Now glorify me, Father, with you, with the glory that I had with you before the world began.

I revealed your name to those whom you gave me out of the world. They belonged to you, and you gave them to me, and they have kept your word. Now they know that everything you gave me is from you, because the words you gave to me I have given to them, and they accepted them and truly understood that I came from you, and they have believed that you sent me. I pray for them. I do not pray for the world but for the ones you have given me, because they are yours, and everything

In His prayer to the Father, Jesus asks to be glorified before the people given to Him by the Father. Jesus gives His followers eternal life, this that they would know the Father as the one true God.

The followers of Jesus are reminded again and again in this gospel that the Father and Jesus are One.

All that Jesus taught the Apostles and through them, all of the faithful, came from the Father, as Jesus, Himself, came from the Father.

of mine is yours and everything of yours is mine, and I have been glorified in them. And now I will no longer be in the world, but they are in the world, while I am coming to you. Holy Father, keep them in your name that you have given me, so that they may be one just as we are. When I was with them I protected them in your name that you gave me, and I guarded them, and none of them was lost except the son of destruction, in order that the scripture might be fulfilled. But now I am coming to you. I speak this in the world so that they may share my joy completely. I gave them your word, and the world hated them, because they do not belong to the world any more than I belong to the world. I do not ask that you take them out of the world but that you keep them from the evil one. They do not belong to the world any more than I belong to the world. Consecrate them in the truth. Your word is truth. As you sent me into the world, so I sent them into the world. And I consecrate myself for them, so that they also may be consecrated in truth.

I pray not only for them, but also for those who will believe in me through their word, so that they may all be one, as you, Father, are in me and I in you, that they also may be in us, that the world may believe that you

As Jesus is preparing to leave the Apostles He prays to the Father for them. It is what Jesus is doing for His followers even today. He is no longer visibly in the world, but His followers are still here and still have to put up with the enemy. This is why it is so important to keep on searching Jesus' words in order that we, His followers, might keep in touch with Him by following through on His commands and wishes. In this way we are assured of His protection and the continued love of His Father.

The followers of Jesus do not belong to the world, as Jesus did not belong to the world. It is important that His followers do not compromise with the world for, in this way, they would be turning their back on Jesus.

Jesus asks the Father to consecrate His Apostles to the truth. Through them, Jesus prays in the same way for His followers.

Jesus, speaking to the Father, asks His protection even for those who will believe in Him through the words of the Apostles and their successors.

sent me. And I have given them the glory you gave me, so that they may be one, as we are one, I in them and you in me, that they may be brought to perfection as one, that the world may know that you sent me, and that you loved them even as you loved me. Father, they are your gift to me. I wish that where I am they also may be with me, that they may see my glory that you gave me, because you loved me before the foundation of the world. Righteous Father, the world also does not know you, but I know you, and they know that you sent me. I made known to them your name and I will make it known, that the love with which you loved me may be in them and I in them.

(1 – 26)

Chapter 18

Put your sword into its scabbard. Shall I not drink the cup that the Father gave me? (11)

I have spoken publicly to the world. I have always taught in a synagogue or in the temple area where all the Jews gather, and in secret I have said nothing. Why ask me? Ask those who heard me what I said to them. They know what I said.

(20 – 21)

If I have spoken wrongly, testify to the wrong; but if I have

This includes the faithful of today. Jesus' prayer continues for His followers of today, pleading for them with the Father, that they be safe and not overcome by the enemy. 5

10

The followers are to be one among themselves as Jesus and the Father are one. Jesus looks for the same intimacy between 15 Himself and each of his followers as that which exists between Himself and the Father.

20

25

30

35

40

spoken rightly, why do you strike me? (23)

My kingdom does not belong to this world. If my kingdom did belong to this world, my attendants [would] be fighting to keep me from being handed over to the Jews. But as it is, my kingdom is not here.... You say I am a king. For this I was born and for this I came into the world, to testify to the truth. Everyone who belongs to the truth listens to my voice.
(36 - 37)

Jesus testifies that His kingdom is not of this world. His followers, therefore, can understand from this that they too are not of this world.

Jesus asserts to Pilate and through him to His followers that He is a King, but not a king of this world.

Chapter 19

You would have no power over me if it had not been given to you from above. For this reason the one who handed me over to you has the greater sin. (11)

Jesus reminds Pilate, and through him, all of His followers that all authority comes from above, from the Father.

Woman, behold, your son. (26)

Behold, your mother. (27)

Chapter 20

Jesus gives His mother to John, and through John, to all mankind. The relationship between Jesus and His mother still continues, and so does the relationship between His mother and all of mankind.

Stop holding on to me, for I have not yet ascended to the Father. But go to my brothers and tell them, 'I am going to my Father and your Father, to my God and your God.' (17)

Peace be with you. As the Father has sent me, so I send you. Receive the holy Spirit.

Jesus sends His Apostles out into the world to do just what He did. He breathes on them the

Whose sins you forgive are forgiven them, and whose sins you retain are retained. (19 – 23)

Put your finger here and see my hands, and bring your hand and put it into my side, and do not be unbelieving, but believe. (27)

Have you come to believe because you have seen me? Blessed are those who have not seen and have believed. (29)

Chapter 21

Feed my lambs. (15)

Tend my sheep. (16)

Feed my sheep. (17)

Amen, amen, I say to you, when you were younger, you used to dress yourself and go where you wanted; but when you grow old, you will stretch out your hands, and someone else will dress you and lead you where you do not want to go.... Follow me. (18 – 19)

Holy Spirit. This Spirit is received by them, but not as powerfully as at Pentecost. Here it was that Jesus gave power to the Apostles to forgive sins, and through them their successors, and through the successors to those onto whom they pass the power.

Jesus chides Thomas for not believing in the reports that he heard about His resurrection.

Jesus reminds Peter that he has to take charge over the rest of the Apostles and over the flock. It goes right along with the power that He has passed on to him by giving him the keys to the kingdom.

Notes

Fr. Stephen Valenta,
OFM Conv.

A Conventual Franciscan for over fifty years, Fr. Stephen has been in touch with every level of life within a variety of ministries.

His years of experience are now shared through his preaching ministry, which takes him to every corner of the world. He is delighted to offer to you his insights that are very relevant in these difficult times in which we live.

Fr. Stephen is the author of the well-known book *Journey From the Head to the Heart and Beyond...*, which is going into its fourth printing. *Journey From the Head to the Heart and Beyond...* was written by Father to be of help to all who are on their own journey struggling to find their way to enjoy the fullness of life which Jesus came on earth to make possible for every person.

Fr. Stephen offers hope to persons of good will who are striving in their daily life to become a more perfect reflection of Jesus. He does this through his travels, as well as, through a wide variety of audio's and videos that cover all your spiritual needs.

For additional information and catalogue, write to or call:

Hearts to heart/Divine Will Ministries
500 Todt Hill Road • Staten Island, NY 10304
Phone: (718) 981-2168 • Fax: (718) 981-2170